Beyond Empowerment

Beyond Empowerment

*A Pilgrimage with the Catholic Campaign
for Human Development*

Jeffry Odell Korgen

ORBIS BOOKS
www.orbisbooks.com

www.orbisbooks.com

Founded in 1970, Orbis Books endeavors to publish works that enlighten the mind, nourish the spirit, and challenge the conscience. The publishing arm of the Maryknoll Fathers and Brothers, Orbis seeks to explore the global dimensions of the Christian faith and mission, to invite dialogue with diverse cultures and religious traditions, and to serve the cause of reconciliation and peace. The books published reflect the views of their authors and do not represent the official position of the Maryknoll Society. To learn more about Maryknoll and Orbis Books, please visit our website at www.maryknollsociety.org.

Copyright © 2015 by Jeffry Odell Korgen

Cover: (A detail from) POWER TO THE PEOPLE, copyright © 2008 by John August Swanson Giclee, www.JohnAugustSwanson.com. 11¼" by 28½".

Published by Orbis Books, Maryknoll, New York 10545-0302.

Queries regarding rights and permissions should be addressed to: Orbis Books, P.O. Box 302, Maryknoll, New York 10545-0302.

Manufactured in the United States of America

Library of Congress Cataloging-in-Publication Data

Korgen, Jeffry Odell.
    Beyond empowerment : a pilgrimage with the Catholic Campaign For Human Development / Jeffry Odell Korgen.
        pages cm
    Includes bibliographical references and index.
    ISBN 978-1-62698-141-6 (pbk.)
    1. Catholic Campaign for Human Development.   2. Church work with the poor —United States.   3. Church work with the poor—Catholic Church.   I. Title.
BX2347.8.P66K67 2015
267'.18273—dc23

                                                                    2015006819

We shall not cease from exploration
And the end of all our exploring
Will be to arrive where we started
And know the place for the first time.
T. S. Eliot, *Four Quartets*

Contents

Acknowledgments

A "cloud of witnesses" helped to develop this book—from identifying a geographic and programmatic diversity of groups to the final copy editing. It would be impossible to thank everyone involved in telling the stories of almost a dozen organizations and the church agency supporting them, simply because they easily number in the hundreds. Thanks to everyone!

That said, I would like to personally thank Ralph McCloud, Catholic Campaign for Human Development's (CCHD's) director, Jonathan Reyes, executive director of the Department of Justice, Peace, and Human Development at the United States Conference of Catholic Bishops, and the U.S. Conference of Catholic Bishops CCHD committee, particularly its chair, the Most Rev. Jaime Soto of the Diocese of Sacramento. CCHD's grants specialists—Randy Keesler, Sean Wendlinder, Sandy Mattingly-Paulen, Kate Dorsett, and Lydia Giles—helped to navigate the unique institutional identities of each project featured.

CCHD diocesan directors Tom Costanza, Rob Gorman, J. L. Drouhard, Joanne Welter, Tom Navin, and Deacon Sam Dunning provided guidance, friendship, and a helping hand before, during, and after interview trips. Comic artist extraordinaire Kevin C. Pyle offered interview assistance and reflective insight during research outings to Texas and Arkansas as well as the beautifully drawn spinoffs *Wage Theft Comics #1* and *Worker Justice Illustrated #2* (available in print from Interfaith Worker Justice). Julie Korgen provided photography and was a great fellow traveler in the Tohono O'odham Nation.

Kudos, thanks, and hugs to each interviewee and organizer—you opened your heart, mind, and soul to me, and I am forever grateful.

Orbis Books and I have now produced three books together. With great admiration, I'd like to thank publisher Robert Ellsberg, who gave time to think through the place of this book in the pantheon of social justice storytelling, and editor Jim Keane, whose attention to detail in the editing process yielded a stronger manuscript.

The copy editing team at Korgen Associates—Dr. Kathleen Odell Korgen and Dr. Patricia Odell—made sure the worst writing never made it out of the house. Beta-testers Kate Dorsett and Susan Kovach both identified important ways to strengthen the manuscript and ensured that many grammatical errors, malapropisms, and wonk-out stat fests filtered out of the final manuscript. Jessica Korgen gave great hugs on my return from research trips and always had the right thing to say on the phone when I had stayed away from home too long.

I can't thank my wife Kathleen enough, so I'll at least do it twice—thank you Kath for supporting dreams like writing this book. You are also a dream come true!

Introduction:
Beyond Empowerment

*Today . . . masses of people find themselves excluded and margin-
alized: without work, without possibilities, without any means of
escape. Human beings are themselves considered consumer goods
to be used and then discarded. . . . It is no longer simply about
exploitation and oppression, but something new. Exclusion ultimately has to do with what it means to be a part of the society
in which we live; those excluded are no longer society's underside
or its fringes or its disenfranchised—they are no longer even a
part of it. The excluded are not the "exploited" but the outcast,
the "leftovers."*

—Pope Francis
The Joy of the Gospel (Evangelii Gaudium), no. 53

In a meeting with journalists immediately after his elevation
to the papacy, Pope Francis stated, "Oh, how I would like a poor
Church, and [a Church] for the poor." At the time, many of us
thought we knew what he meant. We didn't.

Since that press conference in 2013, Francis has consistently
challenged us to understand the meaning of "a poor Church for
the poor." Through his travels and in his speeches and writings,

he has always guided us to the poorest of the poor among the poorest of the poor: "the excluded."

Who are the excluded among us in the United States? Some are hidden, some hidden in plain sight. Maybe they are disabled; maybe they live in a Native American Indian nation. Perhaps they were raised in a "no-parent" family, or they are unauthorized migrants or ex-prisoners. Pope Francis calls us to be a church of and for these excluded people. Isn't it time we got to know them better?

This book is a faith journey with the excluded, guided by the Catholic Campaign for Human Development (CCHD), which funds economic development and organizing among the poorest communities in the United States. Together on pilgrimage, we will travel to south Louisiana to meet the children of Katrina, now grown, who fight poverty, violence, and hopelessness with traditional New Orleans cuisine. We will come to know the people of Bayou Country, whose homes are literally dissolving into the sea, who advocate for coastal restoration in the shadow of cultural genocide. We will hear immigrant women in the Pacific Northwest share their story of victory over the most tenacious of school bullies—a flawed standardized test. Workers from Texas, Arkansas, Minnesota, and California will share their struggles over wage theft and dangerous workplaces—and how they fought back with the help of faith communities. In Chicago's low- and moderate-income suburbs, people with disabilities will describe how they organize to overcome prejudice, condescension, and unemployment. Native Americans in southwest Arizona will offer one solution to the triple challenges of diabetes, vanishing culture, and the moribund economy of an excluded people: traditional native foods. Finally, ex-prisoners in Massachusetts will share their stories of coming together to overcome the "life sentence" of unemployment that a criminal record carries. Along the way, inspired by quotes from the Holy Father to guide our spiritual reflection, we will attend to the most important story of all—the human development fostered by these CCHD-funded organizations.

The Story of CCHD

The U.S. Catholic Bishops founded CCHD in 1970 to help "people who are poor speak and act for themselves."[1] Empowerment is one tool CCHD promotes toward that end, but it is a word that many people define differently. A dictionary might simply define it as "give[ing] power to someone,"[2] but this explanation only raises another question: "What is power?"

In the parlance of organizers who work for CCHD-funded organizations, power is "the ability to act." It's how you get things done in "the world as it is," on your way to fostering "the world as it should be." Veteran organizer Michael Gecan of the Industrial Areas Foundation describes the reason low-income people need to build power:

> Without power, there's no real recognition. They don't even see you. They never learn your name. Without recognition, there's no reciprocity; there's not even a "you" to respond to. And without reciprocity, there's no real relationship of respect. Without power, you can only be a supplicant, a serf, a victim, or a wishful thinker who soon begins to whine. . . . You're going to have to have enough organized people and organized money, enough discipline and enough luck to make it happen. That's the way it works in the world as it is.[3]

Organizers like Gecan teach us that power stems from organized money and organized people. People living in poverty and the institutions to which they belong may be able to cobble together enough money to hire an organizer, but their strength lies in organized people. By building and leveraging their relationships, what sociologists call "social capital," ordinary people living in poverty might turn out hundreds, even thousands of people to a public meeting, thereby influencing a public official or private sector leader. Building those relationships requires, in turn, conducting hundreds, even thousands of one-on-one (1:1) relational meetings over a lifetime.

In CCHD-funded organizations, leaders learn how to conduct 1:1 relational meetings from organizers and other leaders. The organizer leads trainings, facilitates role-playing, and helps leaders debrief these thirty to forty-five-minute meetings. She or he helps a prospective leader to start public conversations, to ask others, "What do you dream of? For this neighborhood? This community? This nation?" "What makes you angry?" "What do you wish for your children?" These can be energizing questions, *empowering* questions for prospective leaders, helping them develop the ability to act in public life.

The organizer then helps the leaders initiate winnable campaigns on specific issues, all the while remembering that her or his role is not to act on behalf of the leaders but to help them develop the ability to act. For CCHD-funded organizations, this is the definition of empowerment and the standard of the stories you are about to read.

But human development does not culminate with empowerment. Integral Human Development, as Pope Francis describes, "engages us at every level of our being."[4] Pope Paul VI coined the term *Integral Human Development* in his 1967 papal encyclical *On the Development of Peoples (Populorum Progressio)*. Pope Paul wanted to break out of the stagnant conversation of his time on development, with its emphasis on economic terms like "per capita income" and "gross national product." Little spiritual, social, or moral vocabulary accompanied these discussions. He wrote *On the Development of Peoples* to present a Catholic alternative. In this letter to the church, one of the highest expressions of papal teaching, Paul VI wrote, "Development . . . cannot be restricted to economic growth alone." Authentic development, the pope insisted, must foster the growth of the *whole* person.[5]

Integral Human Development arises from that bedrock principle of Catholic social teaching—human dignity. The term refers to the human condition as understood by the Catholic Church. We are each made in the image and likeness of God and therefore possess an inherent dignity, no matter where we live, what racial/

ethnic background we come from, how much money we have, how abled or disabled we are, what our sexual or gender orientation is, and so on. If we are human, we possess dignity, given by God. As Pope Francis writes in his apostolic exhortation *The Joy of the Gospel (Evangelii Gaudium),* "No one can strip us of the dignity bestowed upon us by this boundless and unfailing love."[6]

Two other principles of Catholic social teaching figure prominently into Integral Human Development: solidarity and subsidiarity. *Solidarity* is the very basic idea that people are interdependent and responsible for one another. This principle begins to answer the question posed of Jesus in Luke's Gospel: "Who is my neighbor?" (Luke 10:25–37). Explanations of and references to solidarity can be found throughout the major documents of Catholic social teaching. The word appears twenty-seven times in the *Catechism of the Catholic Church,* which describes solidarity as "a direct demand of human and Christian brotherhood."[7]

The concept of solidarity is the Catholic Christian's reply to Cain's question, "Am I my brother's keeper?" Pope Francis, quoting Pope Benedict's insight, "Globalization makes us neighbors, but does not make us brothers,"[8] takes the teaching a step further, calling for a renewed commitment to *fraternity* as a response to the diffidence of Cain.[9] In solidarity we recognize the connection between all humanity; in fraternity we embrace our familial relationship. We are, as Catholic Relief Services reminds us, "One Human Family."

Complementing this vision of solidarity and fraternity is the principle of *subsidiarity,* the notion that the smallest *possible* social unit should take on the challenges of social life. Subsidiarity is like a two-sided coin; referencing Catholic social teaching, some pundits and politicians speak only of one side—that we need to first look to the smallest possible social grouping to solve social problems. But subsidiarity does not end there. What if that social group is unable to solve a problem? A larger social unit must step in (the other side of the coin), still respecting the rights and responsibilities of the first group, but intervening nonetheless. In addition to solidarity and subsidiarity, Catholic social teaching principles such as God's special, but not exclusive, love of the poor; the call to family, community, and participation; rights and responsibilities; the dignity of work and the rights of workers; and the care of God's creation figure prominently into the stories of empowerment and beyond that follow—each a case study of Integral Human Development.

Pope Benedict affirmed Integral Human Development in his 2008 Encyclical, *Charity in Truth* (*Caritas in Veritate*), noting, "The truth of development consists of its completeness: if it does not involve the whole man and every man, it is not true development."[10] Later he laid out the theological rationale for organizing and economic development: promoting, first, "new forms of political participation . . . that have come about through the activity of organizations operating in civil society,"[11] and second, "commercial entities based on mutualist principles and pursuing social ends to take root and express themselves . . . *civilizing the economy* (original italics)."[12] Benedict recommended community organizing and economic development as two means by which people living in poverty might come to participate in decisions affecting their families and communities.

Each November, in parishes throughout the United States, Catholics contribute to an annual collection supporting CCHD's grant making to community organizing and economic development organizations led by people living in poverty. Local bishops send three-fourths of the collection to the national CCHD office, and one-fourth stays in their diocese to be used for local poverty alleviation efforts. In 2013, the CCHD national office received almost $10 million in contributions, distributing about $7 million to 157 organizing projects and close to $2 million to 37 economic development ventures.

We now begin our pilgrimage with the CCHD, traveling throughout the United States to meet "the excluded." We will visit ten different areas of the country, with each church-funded organization presenting a unique response to poverty, and each offering its story of what happens when the assets of the church come together with the assets of people living in poverty. Along the way, brief quotations of Pope Francis will spiritually frame what we are about to experience.

We embark on our journey in a state beloved in the public imagination, sustained by a boom in reality television shows. But we are about to experience a different kind of reality show involving Louisiana—the state with the second-highest poverty rate in the nation—and New Orleans—the city with the second-highest murder rate. Our first stop is an award-winning restaurant and economic development project where young adults scarred by disasters and murder prepare a table of reconciliation to which all are welcome—Café Reconcile.

Chapter 1

A Place at the Table:
Café Reconcile and Bayou Interfaith

Geographer Peirce Lewis once described New Orleans as "an inevitable city on an impossible site."[1] Ever-present street violence and the trauma of Katrina relocations have introduced new levels of impossibility to the lives of Crescent City young adults, many of whom live in poverty. To the west, Native American fisher folk and their African American and Cajun neighbors watch as their land dissolves into the Gulf of Mexico—the consequences of adapting the waterways and shore for commerce—and wonder if their home, too, is an "impossible site."

Here we begin our pilgrimage across the United States, where America as we know it began, decades before Plymouth Rock, as Hernando de Soto bullied his way past Choctaws through the Mississippi Delta looking for gold, followed by French trappers and colonists, more Spaniards, African slaves and free persons of color, remnants of displaced tribes, Creole French and Haitians fleeing that island's slave rebellion, Acadians (Cajuns) expelled from Canada, and American colonists looking to join the booming economy. These founders created a uniquely American civilization, often described as a rich gumbo of cultural ingredients. It is a society now threatened from within by poverty and violence and from the outside by climate change.

Many Louisiana residents living in poverty, like so many others you will meet in this book, have been systematically excluded

9

from the table of public life for reasons not only of race, but also class. They are Pope Francis's portion of the poor, "the excluded." Organizing themselves in Catholic Campaign for Human Development (CCHD)-funded economic development and organizing projects, some of these leaders have responded not with bitterness or the language of victimhood. They have instead called for a place at the table of public life where decisions are made about flood control, coastal restoration, and disaster response through Bayou Interfaith Shared Community Organizing (BISCO), and also built a dinner table, ornamented with the best food New Orleans has to offer, a feast to which all are welcome—Café Reconcile (or Café).

Emeril Lagasse spends time with Café Reconcile students.

Katrina's Children Come of Age

Our generation will show that it can rise to the promise found in each young person when we know how to give them space. This means that we have to create the material and spiritual conditions for their full development; to give them a solid basis on which to build their lives; to guarantee their safety and their education to be everything they can be; to pass on to them lasting values that make life worth living; to give them a transcendent horizon for their thirst for authentic happiness and their creativity for the good; to give them the legacy of a world worthy of human life; and to awaken in them their greatest potential as builders of their own destiny, sharing responsibility for the future of everyone. If we can do all this, we anticipate today the future that enters the world through the window of the young.

—Pope Francis
World Youth Day Welcome Ceremony, July 22, 2013

Twenty-two-year-old Brian Davis counted on the fingers of his right hand, mouthing the names of friends who had been murdered over the last two years. He moved to his left hand, then back to his right, then back once again—four hands in all. "Twenty," he said. "Twenty friends or family that I was close to, I lost."

Asked to share a story about someone special, Brian began with Lanesha, a friend whom he called a sister; they were that close. It was Lanesha who first told him about Café Reconcile. He began, "She told me, 'You got to come to Café Reconcile, because it helps you a lot. It puts you in a great job, where you need to be. It can help you a lot with goal setting and all that.'"

Lanesha knew well the benefits of Café Reconcile. She completed the life skills and culinary training offered by the fifteen-year-old nonprofit, excelled in a three-week internship, and then secured a living-wage job in the high end of New Orleans's revived hospitality industry. Then, sitting inside a car in her uptown New Orleans neighborhood, she was cut down by a string of bullets in a gang battle over drug territory.

Grief hit Brian hard, but he found a way to honor Lanesha's memory. He enrolled in Café Reconcile's fifteen-month program where he learns life skills, participates in group and individual counseling, and practices positive work habits. Lanesha is always present. "I got to keep her word and stay here," he said.

At Café Reconcile, Brian expected to learn how to cook; he knew little of the culinary world except the difference between a pot and a pan. But the most challenging—and exciting—dimension of Café Reconcile for Brian was the life skills training. In the first three weeks, students focus on the "soft skills" that make people employable, which Café Reconcile calls "The 8 Habits of Success." These disciplines include (1) be on time; (2) be present all day, every day; (3) accept and follow direction; (4) work well with others, even when it's difficult; (5) have a positive, not negative, attitude towards the work; (6) take care of personal appearance every day; (7) get things done within the expected time; and (8) do a quality job at each and every task. The 8 Habits were derived from the "21st Century Success Principles," developed by the New Orleans Jobs Initiative over a ten-year period to address participant understanding of workplace culture. The 8 Habits are especially geared toward African American youth with little prior connection to the job market.

Café Reconcile staff members understand that for their students, developing the 8 Habits of Success is more than a matter of willpower—peer support and good role models are essential. Along with the intense life skills classes that take place for three weeks, men's and women's empowerment groups meet three times per week in that time period. Brian attends both individual and group counseling with Onassis Jones, a licensed therapist and an ordained minister, to help him understand and overcome emotional obstacles to success. "Mr. Onassis helped me," he said, "just telling me to calm down. They got a thing. It's called 'The Hot Button,' where when you get real mad, you're on this hot button. He just tells me, 'Calm down. Get off the hot button.'"

Put yourself in Brian's shoes. Would you have any emotional obstacles, any baggage, if twenty of your friends and family were killed over a two-year period? Might you suffer from depression, have difficulty concentrating, or "get on the hot button" at inappropriate times? I notice Brian's absence of emotion during our interview—it appears that he is not feeling much as he tells me about the murders and the people he lost. It's all there, though. Onassis is helping Brian to express his grief in appropriate ways and shift gears when the emotions come out in behaviors that will make him unemployable.

Onassis describes his counseling paradigm as cognitive behaviorism, helping young people think through the possible outcomes of every situation they encounter and choose the healthiest response. When students arrive at Reconcile, he conducts an intake interview, identifying psychiatric, legal, and substance abuse histories, family of origin dynamics, and religious involvement. He believes that somewhere between a quarter and a third of Reconcile students live with a serious mental illness, while about 70 percent have substance abuse issues. He is also acutely aware of the spiritual challenges present, just beneath the emotional and psychiatric issues. All students take a drug test upon acceptance, but failing it does not disqualify them from participation; it is for diagnostic purposes—to assess their baseline issues. When it comes time for their internships to begin, nine weeks later, they must be clean.

Onassis disdains the medicalization of all behavior problems, but he believes in helping students with serious mental illnesses become medication compliant. Taking proper medications and becoming free of illegal drugs is just the first step, however. The most profound challenge is helping youth and young adults deal with the breakdown of family and the many traumas in their lives, including one-parent families, no-parent families, and two-parent families in which the young person feels utterly isolated. For many survivors of street violence and Hurricane Katrina, Posttraumatic Stress Disorder (PTSD) is an issue. Even a heavy rainfall might trigger their addictions. Onassis's group and individual counseling sessions help Reconcile students make better choices.

For Brian, choosing to turn away from smoking marijuana when he felt overcome by grief was the first step. "When I started grieving and all of that," he said, "I was like, 'I need to smoke!' And they'd talk to me and they'd be like, 'No. That ain't good. Just talk about the situation and you'll be good.' That helped a lot, too." Also, one of Brian's greatest assets—his quick wit—could have been an obstacle. "Sometimes I can act like I'm clowning around when it's time to be serious," he said. Clowning might provide him with release and affirmation, but it put Brian's employability at risk and distracted him from dealing with his feelings about losing so many friends to gun violence. Talking about the emotions underneath the clowning helped Brian succeed at work, despite his personal losses.

Loss is a way of life for the children of Katrina. In addition to the Crescent City's constant din of violence, nearly all of the sixteen- to twenty-two-year-old Café Reconcile participants survived the hurricane only to be evacuated long term. Ernetta Hall, Brian's nineteen-year-old classmate, shared her story of relocating to Baton Rouge after losing her home and dog in Gentilly, an eastern New Orleans neighborhood. The traumatized family never fit in and never moved on. "After almost a year, my mother said, 'This place is not for us—we should go back home,'" she recalled. Jobless for months, Ernetta's mother moved the family into a friend's cramped home, waiting for the devastated New Orleans economy to revive.

Today, Café Reconcile provides Ernetta with a reliable structure to her life, helping her disassociate from negative influences and strengthen ties with positive people in her life. She explained, "The streets will take you places you have never been before. It's difficult. People will try to drag you into selling drugs, smoking weed." Upon reflection, Ernetta realized she had two types of friends—those who encouraged her to grow into a new life, like the Café Reconcile graduate who relentlessly pushed her to enroll in the program—and those who tried to pull her back into a routine of sleeping all day, smoking marijuana, and working minimum wage jobs just to get by.

"This girl I know was like, 'Why you going to the Café?'" she recalled. "'They only pay you $50 a week. They tell you that you can't smoke. You've got to tie your hair back, and all that.' I'm like, 'So? I'm doing it for me. This is what I want to do. It's going to better myself.' She was always telling me down stuff. So I was like, 'You know what? I'm just going to stop talking to you, because I feel like you're not being a good friend.' She was like, 'Well, I'm just saying. They're not paying you enough. You can go and work at McDonald's and they'll pay you this much.' I was like, 'I don't want to work at McDonald's. I worked for McDonald's. It's not for me. This is what I want to do, and I'm going to do it. I'm going to finish the program.'"

Reconcile staff believe most every student comes to this crossroads—when friends stuck in dysfunctional patterns try to prevent them from changing unhealthy habits. In life skills classes, Onassis presents the image of crabs in a pot: "The fire is on, and a crab is trying to get up, but there's some crabs trying to bring them down," he explained. Students immediately relate to the image. Often, the only option is to "divorce their friends," as Ernetta did. Brian began to do so as well, tough for a popular young man, but essential to turning his life in a positive direction. "I stopped being with friends who look like they're dangerous, like they play with guns or sell drugs," he said. "I don't deal with all that no more. I'm just with my family now. I just be inside."

Ernetta described some of the changes she made as result of the training—including how she spoke. "I learned how to talk with inside people," she said, "instead of how I talk to my friends." At Café Reconcile, this is called "code switching," changing one's speech based on the immediate social context. Street slang is for the streets; polite standard English is for the workplace. "Some customers," she said, "they'd be like, 'How are you doing?' And I'm like 'Fine, and you?' but to my friends, I'd say, 'Hey, girl!'"

When Ernetta began to integrate both manners of speaking into her personal life, friends reacted negatively. She explained, "They be like, 'Girl, why you talking like that? You should talk how you regular talk!' I'm like, "This is how I talk. I can't help it." I used to say the N-word. But now I be like 'boys' or 'young men.'"

Ernetta quickly learned that code switching is not relegated to speech. In life skills classes, she practiced looking customers in the eye, an action that might be seen as a provocation in her neighborhood. Shaking hands, a symbol of business relationships, was a practice she had generally ignored. Why bother when hugs and kisses would do? She practiced firm handshakes with her classmates, and when she greeted me prior to our interview, she put her learning into practice like an old pro. Even signals like posture came up for discussion. After a lifetime of slouching, Ernetta learned that potential employers might misinterpret her laid-back appearance as a sign of laziness. Following the training, she corrected her posture to sit up straight—at least on the job. Brian explained, "In the life skills classes, they tell you, 'You're always on a stage. Someone is always watching.'"

At the beginning of her training, Ernetta gave up smoking marijuana just to pass the drug test. Now she has simply lost the desire to smoke—or sleep all day and eat junk food, for that matter. "Since I came to Café Reconcile, I do stuff," she said. "I run around the block two or three times. I engage with my brothers and sisters a little more. I do stuff I wouldn't normally do. I read books."

Ernetta is currently reading, for the second time, *The Skin I'm In*, by Sharon G. Flake, about a high school girl teased for her appearance and homemade clothes. Inspired by a teacher with a skin disease who remains supremely self-confident, she stays in school, ignores her detractors, and becomes a famous designer.

Ernetta notices that her younger brothers now look up to her (she is the middle child among nine brothers and sisters) in a way that she never experienced toward her older siblings. "My little brothers," she said, "every day they'd be like 'Netta, how was your day? I want to work where you work!' The youngest, he's only four years old. I figure I was doing good by that."

The following day, Ernetta, Brian, and their eighteen class-mates entered the Café at 8:00 a.m. as usual, eating a hot break-fast served by the staff (homemade waffles with breakfast sausage corn dogs, served alongside freshly cut fruit, orange juice, and P. J.'s Coffee with chicory) and discussing "the word of the day." Today's word: *Determination*. Newly elected City Councilman Jason R. Williams, a former Tulane University football star who is now lead counsel for his own law firm, offered a reflection. First, he asked the group how they would define determination. Brian responded, "I feel like determination is to a human being what gas is to a car. It'll keep you running."

"You hit the nail on the head," Councilman Williams said, "but then you've got to decide which direction the car is going to go." Ernetta and Brian lean in—they know something of this word, *determination*. They have shown a *determination* to break the cycle of poverty by facing the traumas of death and relocation head-on, developing life skills, switching codes, divorcing friends who hold them back, clawing at them like crabs in a bucket. They have immersed themselves in the jambalaya of flavors that is New Orleans cuisine and the new world of professional hospitality for six weeks at Reconcile.

Their *determination* shone as they learned new kitchen skills. Brian sautéed vegetables for the first time and discovered that not only does he enjoy preparing vegetables this way, he's good at it; Ernetta shared her newly found talent for cooking chicken-fried steaks with her proud father, who always dreamed of being a chef (He responded, "I've never fried a steak. It is so good. I should have fried steak a long time ago! They taught you how to cook the gumbo yet?").

Both Brian and Ernetta acknowledged that *determination* is something they want more of. It has carried them this far—but more is necessary. Ernetta recounted an experience with learning to fry chicken. "We were flipping the stuff," she said, "and I was like 'I'm scared I'm going to burn myself!' So [graduate trainer] Irivanne was like, 'Girl, you're not going to burn yourself. Just try.' And I flipped it! And then the flame was going up, and I was like, 'I'm a real chef!'" She said, "You're not a chef yet, but you're getting there." With *determination*, both Ernetta and Brian will.

The Challenge:
Violence, Inequality, Racism, and Recovery

When, in 1992, lifelong New Orleans resident Craig Cuccia turned his life over to Jesus Christ in front of thousands of other Catholics, he saw a city in need of reconciliation: between blacks and whites and among the haves and the have-nots. The thirty-four-year-old businessman had done well in the oil business, in the construction trade, and with rental properties. He was wealthy by many measures, but Craig felt spiritually bankrupt. At a Charismatic Catholic convention, Bishop Sam Jacobs of the Diocese of Houma-Thibodaux gave an altar call, saying, "Jesus Christ was a fool—would you be willing to be a fool for Jesus Christ?" Craig felt as if Bishop Jacobs was speaking to him personally, and stepped up to the altar, offering his life as a "Fool for Christ."

Thus began one response to the poverty, racism, and violence of New Orleans, where the murder rate most years surpasses that of any other U.S. city except Detroit, and the poverty index remains mired at over 27 percent. Black poverty is double the white rate in the Crescent City, where nearly half of African American men are unemployed. African American men who are working earn about half the salary white men make: $31,018 and $60,075, annually. Almost half of African American households earn less than $20,000 per year.[2] These statistics are the sad legacy of a city torn by slavery, segregation, and racism for centuries.

It was within this context of hurt and conflict that Craig began to meet with Fr. Emile LaFrance, who encouraged him to go into full-time ministry, running a soup kitchen and a thrift store.

After Fr. Emile's death from cancer three years later, Craig began to meet for spiritual direction with Fr. Harry Thompson, a Jesuit priest with a knack for nonprofit start-ups. Those conversations led to a dialogue joined by Craig's brother-in-law, Tim Falcon, on the nature and potential application of reconciliation in New Orleans, given the many issues of race and class facing the city. They took as their inspiration the following passage in St. Paul's Second Letter to the Corinthians:

Brothers and sisters:
Whoever is in Christ is a new creation:
The old things have passed away;
Behold, new things have come.
And all this is from God,
Who has reconciled us to himself through Christ
And given us the ministry of reconciliation,
Namely, God was reconciling the world to himself in Christ,
Not counting their trespasses against them
And entrusting to us, the message of reconciliation.
So we are ambassadors for Christ,
As if God were appealing through us.
We implore you on behalf of Christ,
Be reconciled to God.
For our sake he made him to be sin who did not know sin,
So that we might become the righteousness of God in him.
—*2 Corinthians 5:17–21*[3]

In 1996, Craig purchased the building where Café Reconcile is now housed for $50,000, smack in the middle of New Orleans's leading hotspot for murder and drug dealing. A prototype youth program, orienting young people to culinary careers and introducing them to African American professionals, was the first effort housed in the building, succeeded in 2000 by Café Reconcile, with funding from CCHD and technical assistance from Tom Costanza, CCHD's local director in the Archdiocese of New Orleans.

Craig served as executive director from 2000 to 2008, and then turned over the reins to others who developed the Café Reconcile model into what it is today. Along the way, Café Reconcile added more training in life skills, more counseling, more mentoring. Today, Glen Armantrout, former chairman of the board of the Louisiana Restaurant Association and chief operating officer of the Acme Oyster House, leads the organization and spearheads its expansion plan. The "New" Reconcile New Orleans will include 75 percent more Café seating, kitchen upgrades, double the capacity to train students, opportunities to serve both breakfast and dinner in addition to lunch, and expanded training and office space. Thanks to patronage by Chef Emeril Lagasse and Chef John Besh, as well as many other local individuals and businesses, the Café is poised to build a substantial addition to its table of reconciliation.

From Hot Sauce Land to Hoboken

The Café Reconcile student experience is one of constantly opening new doors, and, with a mix of fear and excitement, stepping into new worlds: Ernetta flipping fried chicken. Brian sautéing vegetables. Both confront the obstacles of unrelenting grief and trauma; both leave behind friends who tug at their arms, imploring, "Don't move forward! Don't leave me!"

But once students complete their internships and begin their first jobs in the higher tiers of the hospitality industry, what new doors lie ahead? How high can they set their sights? Chris Okorie, an early Reconcile grad, provides a glimpse into possible next steps for Brian and Ernetta.

Like most Reconcile participants, Chris was a long-term Katrina evacuee, placed in "Hot Sauce Land," New Iberia, Louisiana, the home of Tabasco, with his grandmother and mother. Chris's mother died several months after the move, from an ailment she contracted immediately after the storm. It took five years to rebuild his grandmother's home in uptown New

Orleans. By then, Chris and his grandmother had grown weary of Hot Sauce Land and just wanted to get back home.

Upon returning to New Orleans, Chris drifted. Jobs were just beginning to come back, but who would hire a twenty-year-old high school graduate with no work experience? The answer came from an unlikely source.

Chris and his best friend were sitting on his grandmother's porch, playing games and talking. "So this homeless guy came up to us," he recalled. "And he knew that me and my friend had been hanging out on the porch for a while because I didn't have a job at the time, and neither did my friend. He just kind of walked up to us and told us about this program that could help us kind of do something with our lives. Because we were both kind of desperate at the time, me and him. So my friend went into Reconcile, and I followed behind him, after he graduated, in 2010. I wasn't really expecting a whole lot because I really had nothing to lose at the time. I was very fortunate, because of what I got out of it at the end—it was very much a career."

Like many graduates—even the most talented, Chris had no interest in the culinary arts before his training at the Café. "I pretty much learned that I had a passion for something that I didn't really know I had a passion for, and that was cooking," he said. The life skills classes and counseling helped him develop the attitude and behaviors he would need to turn that passion into a career. After an internship as a "food runner," the person who literally runs a covered tray from a restaurant kitchen to its dining room server, Chris got back into the kitchen at Café Adelaide, under the wing of sous chef Orlando Harris.

Chef Orlando's own life story impacted Chris personally. He had grown up on the same streets of New Orleans and been in and out of jail several times before he turned his life around. "A lot of the things he went through, I had to go through," Chris recalled. "He showed us that you can pretty much change your life, and let this [cooking] be your stepping stone, the door in."

Chris threw himself into work at Café Adelaide, attracting the attention of the John Besh Foundation, which awarded him its 2012 Chefs Move! Scholarship for minority chefs. The scholarship provided him with ten months of certificate study at the International Culinary Center (ICC) in New York City and field work at cutting-edge restaurants in nearby Hoboken, New Jersey, along with a computer, media training, and living expenses. Chef John Besh established the scholarship in 2011 to help ensure that chefs of color would become better represented at the highest levels of Louisiana kitchen leadership.

The ICC experience opened up another world for Chris. "I pretty much hadn't been outside of Louisiana my entire life," he said. "To get a chance to go to school for ten months and see different things and learn and progress my career, you can't really use another word besides life-changing. That's something I can carry with me the rest of my life." Horizons opened further later that year, when Chris won "Best Chef Under 25" and a fellowship to Italy for three weeks of study, tasting, and cooking. These scholarships did what they were intended to do—Chris has now set a ten-year vision to become an executive chef, building on his current position as sauté cook at Café Adelaide. He hopes to move up to sous chef in the next five years as an intermediate step. For a young man who just wanted a job—any job—five years ago, Café Reconcile has taught him the life skills needed to succeed and launched him on a journey that may take him to the top of restaurant leadership. A leadership position like executive chef would, of course, lift Chris from his start in poverty into the upper middle class, but it would also be part of a return of African Americans to leadership in a style of cooking founded by their forefathers and mothers, the French Creoles.

This latter accomplishment returns us to the original purpose of the Café—reconciliation. But not everyone, all the time, has such lofty goals in mind. Sometimes people involved in Café Reconcile are just trying to run a restaurant or hotel—and that's why the program works.

Memo from Personnel

Back in 2004, Ray Bruce had not enlisted to become a soldier in anyone's War on Poverty—he was just doing his job. The New Orleans Loew's Hotel personnel director needed to find and hire entry-level cooks, but he soon ran into difficulty. The city's hospitality industry was well into its recovery, but cooks with the right skills were hard to find. A colleague at another hotel suggested he try Café Reconcile, which had a growing reputation for producing home-grown culinary talent.

As a means of getting to know potential interns, Bruce offered them a tour of the luxury Loew's hotel so they could see what high-end hospitality looked like. Several had never even ridden on an elevator. One student asked, "Do you think I could work here?" Bruce replied, "Yes, but you've got to earn it. We'll meet you halfway."

That young man, Raynard Janeau, was determined to escape the violence and poverty of the city's Seventh Ward. Like many of his peers, he had grown up poor, lost friends to street violence, and still bore the emotional scars of Katrina. Raynard made a point of shaking Bruce's hand and thanked him for the tour. That handshake and expression of gratitude became a daily routine for the next month, after he was selected to intern at Loew's.

Raynard began preparing salads and desserts. Each day he made a point to interact with Bruce, shaking his hand and thanking him for the internship. When the internship ended, he was hired. Over the next four years he worked his way up to cooking soups, then entrees. His current wage, $11.75/hour, produces an annual income of about $27,000–30,000, with overtime, well into living wage territory for a single man with no dependents. In 2014, at the age of twenty-seven, he purchased a home. He also just became licensed as a part-time barber to supplement his income further. Raynard credits two key elements of Café Reconcile's training for his accomplishments—"The 8 Habits of Success" and "code switching," both described above. Like Brian and Ernetta, he also had to make choices about the company he would keep, retaining those who reinforced the positive messages learned at Reconcile and leaving behind the others.

Bruce is clearly proud of Raynard's accomplishments as an employee, but, he adds, "As a New Orleanian, I want people to succeed and get off the street. I see Café Reconcile as helping people to do that. For me it's worth all my time and effort if I can help just one person—and we've helped several. And someone like Raynard has purchased a home."

Beyond Empowerment I

Personnel directors like Ray Bruce have developed an abiding respect for Café Reconcile, but so have prominent chefs and philanthropists Emeril Lagasse and John Besh. So, too, have politicians like Jason R. Williams, all the way up to Mayor Mitch Landrieu and former Senator Mary Landrieu. Immediately after Hurricane Katrina, Café Reconcile was one of only twelve restaurants to reopen, providing a place to meet and greet for the leaders of the city's nonprofit community and public sector while feeding hungry construction workers and volunteers. Post-Katrina, Café Reconcile became a symbolic dinner table for the entire community.

Today, the Café continues to host that table of reconciliation, but its leaders and graduates have also secured places at the table of public life, where the future of New Orleans is discussed, bringing voices previously silenced to the conversation. What began as a prayerful meeting between "Fool for Christ" Craig Cuccia and his spiritual shepherd became not only a tool to fight poverty, but also a means of reconciliation. In the end, reconciliation and ultimately peace will be the greatest fruit of CCHD's investments to combat poverty and violence in the Crescent City. But as most any resident of Louisiana will tell you, there is more to the state than New Orleans. We now travel west to Bayou Country, where a determined group of people living at or near poverty levels have come together to fight an external enemy, a force that destroys a football field of land every hour[4] and, coupled with global climate change, may annihilate entire cultures: coastal erosion.

BISCO: Voice of the Bayou

The book of Genesis tells us that God created man and woman, entrusting them with the task of filling the earth and subduing it, which does not mean exploiting it, but nurturing and protecting it, caring for it through their work.

—Pope Francis
General Audience, Feast of St. Joseph
the Worker, May 1, 2013

Coy Verdin and David Gauthe point out severely eroded areas of the Louisiana coastline.

Coy Verdin cut the motor of his small shrimping boat and we sat silently, appreciating the vastness of the waters. The tiny waves of Terrebonne Bay lapped the side of the boat. "When I was a boy, this was all land," he said, interrupting the quiet and pointing at the water. "We used to hunt over there, and the amount of land here was triple what you see today." Coy's people, the United Houma Nation, are an offshoot of the Choctaw tribe who came to south Louisiana three hundred years ago as French settlers began to populate central Louisiana. They developed practices for catching shrimp and crab in the bayous and bays that Coy still uses today.

Coy joined BISCO seven years ago at the urging of his wife Pam, who attended a BISCO Green Party, a gathering of women who shared ideas on making inexpensive, nontoxic cleaners at the Terrebonne Parish Library in Montegut, Louisiana. While learning about "green cleaning," Pam met BISCO organizers, who invited the couple to attend an ecumenical meeting of church leaders to discuss the needs of the community. As this gathering concerned the 2010 British Petroleum (BP)/Deepwater Horizon oil spill, Coy had a lot to say.

"The oil spill was pretty bad for our area because shrimp and crab fishing areas were always closing and opening," he explained. "I tried to help by talking to fishermen, to see what's going on and to try to get them involved, not just staying inside and waiting for information. No one has ever organized the fishermen before."

The oil spill came at the worst possible time—April, just as crab season began. Trapping areas were closed, and fishermen lost not only their catch, but also their equipment—the crab traps. A long period of clean-up and claims against BP began. BISCO held community meetings, inviting BP officials to explain how they would settle these disaster claims. At first, BISCO saw their mission as holding BP accountable for its role in destroying the local ecology and economy. BISCO executive director Sharon Gauthe, a longtime leader who became a professional organizer, explained how that function evolved into protecting the lives of BP officials.

At one public meeting, a BP executive had finished explaining the claims process when a fisherman rose and strode to the front of the room. Attendees froze—what would he do? Sharon intercepted him, holding the fisherman in a tight embrace, and asserted, live microphone in hand, how wonderful it was that the people of Bayou Country could keep a Christian tone in these difficult meetings. Applause filled the room, and he sat down.

The fisherman later thanked Sharon for stopping him. He felt as if he had lost all self-control and was outside his body watching someone else. There was no telling what he might have done, he said, if Sharon had not intervened. BP officials began to take BISCO more seriously after the incident, looking toward the organization of nineteen "covenant churches" as honest brokers who could bring together victims of the oil spill for productive conversations with the oil company. The grateful executive began to see BISCO as a partner in recovery rather than an adversary.

Organizers describe BISCO's role in the recovery effort as that of a "mediating institution." Individuals like Coy could never go up against BP alone. Jesus's "least of these" and Pope Francis's "excluded" only find an effective voice when they can unite the power of all of the seemingly powerless people into an organization that can both speak for and be accountable to them. Coy's participation is a definitive example—BISCO provided him with an opportunity to speak directly to BP executives, but as a leader he needed BISCO organizers to help develop his public speaking, organizing, and media skills.

The oil industry's impact on the civil parishes (akin to counties) of south Louisiana cannot be overstated. The BP/Deepwater Horizon oil spill was a tremendous setback to everyone in the bayou region, especially to low-income Houma fishermen. The seeds for catastrophe were sown by the oil industry and its partners in government long ago, as various waterways were widened and straightened to let commercial watercraft traverse the region. As a result, today, significant portions of Louisiana face a threat beyond any they have faced in the state's colorful history: disappearing into the ocean.

The Challenge:
From Swimming Pools to Coastal Erosion

BISCO did not start out as an environmental organization, nor would its members describe it so today. Like most congregation-based community organizations, BISCO focuses on member concerns, whatever those issues might be. Not long after its mid-1990s founding, BISCO's greatest concern was the well-being of area youth. Its leaders insisted that low-income children have access to some of the same recreation opportunities as middle-class kids. Through research into city of Thibodaux budgets and scores of 1:1 relational meetings and house meetings (small gatherings at a leader's home or a house of worship) throughout the membership of its covenant churches, BISCO leaders encouraged hundreds of people to attend large public meetings and secured municipal commitments to create a free swimming lesson program for low-income children while expanding Thibodaux's youth recreation program.

Among the key leaders in BISCO's youth campaign was Eloise Taylor, known as Miss Eloise to almost everyone in the organization. Raised by her grandparents on a sugarcane farm in nearby Raceland, Miss Eloise always had a soft spot in her heart for children who needed extra nurturing. Childless herself, she raised eighteen foster children over a period of sixteen years and discovered BISCO's youth campaign to be an excellent public vehicle for her passion for kids. Mostly, Miss Eloise shunned the spotlight. She was always the quiet, dependable leader in the background, where she preferred to stay. That changed when she became involved in what was, for her, the most unlikely of issues: coastal erosion and climate change.

Soon after Hurricanes Katrina and Rita roared through south Louisiana in the fall of 2005, the rest of the country seemed ready to move on. An aid package focused on the urgent issue of housing stalled in Congress, and the Gulf disasters seemed forgotten—at least outside of the Gulf States. BISCO sent a contingent of leaders to Washington, DC, joining other Louisiana, Mississippi, Alabama, and Florida community spokespersons to tell their stories and express local needs to members of Congress. Miss Eloise attended, expecting to play a backup role.

Early in the morning, Miss Eloise appeared for the first meeting of the day with a senator from the Midwest. As she waited outside his office for her partner, a coordinator for the speakout arrived, frantic. "You know, Miss Eloise," she said, "the other woman didn't show up, so you're going to have to talk." She took a deep breath and responded, "Huh? No, *you're* going to talk." The coordinator refused, "No, I'm not supposed to say anything—just bring you to the different offices. You're going to have to talk today."

"Oh, my God!" Miss Eloise said, looking up, praying, "Lord, let some words come out." She entered the senator's office hesitantly to tell the story of life in Thibodaux, the tremendous devastation, the widespread homelessness, and the need for a comprehensive housing bill. The senator listened attentively, and responded, "Oh, we never heard of this before. We're going to look into it."

Miss Eloise continued her unlikely speaking tour, visiting four members of Congress in one day. "And I enjoyed it," she recalled, with a blend of surprise and triumph in her voice. "BISCO's got me all out, to find out what was going on, and learn how to go about, how to present yourself to people and how you could go and help people with different issues." She stood as a proud graduate of what we might call the BISCO School of Public Life, where a person like Miss Eloise can develop both the skills and the courage to sit at the table with a U.S. senator and advocate on the issues most dear to her.

Passage of the Gulf Coast Hurricane Housing Recovery Act of 2007 proved to be most instructive for Miss Eloise and the other BISCO leaders who traveled to Washington in 2005. Similar bills died in Congress that year and in the following session of Congress. Ultimately, however, through the persistence of these leaders, Congress appropriated $2.8 billion for housing assistance in the storm-ravaged areas.

For Miss Eloise, the experience widened the scope of issues she would engage, taking on environmental issues like disaster relief, flood insurance, and coastal erosion. Her self-interests broadened through dialogue with other leaders, both storm victims and wetland area residents. "I really wish they could protect the wetlands from erosion," she said, "bring it back and get it to be solid."

This evolving of consciousness on environmental issues was a common theme among BISCO leaders. Initial concerns about public safety and youth led to concrete victories, more 1:1 and leadership dialogues, and an emerging awareness of the urgency of environmental issues.

Al Carter began his journey with BISCO in the early 2000s while he was still a lieutenant working with Lafourche Parish Sheriff Craig Webre. Immediately prior to a meeting with BISCO, Sheriff Webre appointed Al the official sheriff's liaison to the church organization.

"All of these high-powered police offices, fighting crime, they've got to be one of the most macho groups of people I've ever met," he said. "[But], when Sharon and the BISCO leaders walked in, they took over the entire meeting. They were like, 'Okay, this is what we need to do. This is the timeline in which we're going to do it. This is what we need of you.' When they left, the sheriff looked at me and said, 'Whatever she asks you, just go ahead and do it.' I was impressed. I was like, 'Wait a minute. How did this group of people just take over this meeting?'"

In 2006, Al completed his master's degree in education and began working for the Lafourche Parish School System as an instructor in its Juvenile Justice Center. He joined BISCO through Living Water Baptist Church and quickly learned the answer to his initial question: building relationships through 1:1 meetings and via these relationships developing the ability to act—power. Al reflected on his evolving understanding of power:

At one time, I would think that groups like the Congressional Black Caucus had power, or the Republican Caucus had power. The city council may have power. But I really didn't feel that the little neighborhood groups had that much power. I've learned that that's not necessarily true. I've learned that true power comes from when people get together, focusing on a goal, and push it to the point that they can accomplish something good.

The power of organized people, combined with the discipline of running meetings like those with Sheriff Webre, produced results at the local level: the swimming program, expanded recreation for youth, new kinds of policing—but the impact of hurricanes Katrina and Rita would test the limits of BISCO's power, as the housing bill faltered and then ultimately inched forward to passage.

Al and Miss Eloise championed the issue of housing after the storms, just as new conversations emerged within BISCO regarding the causes of the extreme weather. But BISCO leaders also noted the scientific projection, discussed everywhere throughout Bayou Country, that with fewer barrier islands and coastal wetlands left to weaken storms as they came ashore, the future was one of more and stronger hurricane impacts. "I dealt with the issue of homelessness," Al said, "but the reality is, if we don't do something about coastal erosion, we're *all* going to be homeless."

Local People—Local Solutions

Coastal erosion is without question the greatest challenge BISCO has ever faced, eclipsing even its work with BP. According to a U.S. Geological Survey report, each year between 1985 and 2010, sixteen and a half square miles of Louisiana disappeared into the Gulf of Mexico. This erosion included much of the Isle de Jean Charles, a small island once populated by one hundred Houma Native American families. Now, only twenty-five households remain, including one of the founders of BISCO, Fr. Roch Naquin of the Diocese of Houma-Thibodeaux.

Fr. Roch lives on the island in retirement, dwelling in his family's ancestral home, jacked fourteen feet into the air, above the storm surges. From Fr. Roch's porch, one can see acres of dead trees, killed by salt water intrusion. Eerie forests like this one dot Louisiana's Bayou Country, a harbinger of more death to come.

Leadership runs in Fr. Roch's family. His great-great-grand-father Jean Charles founded the island settlement, and he helped found BISCO, laying the groundwork for the organization in the late 1980s. As Fr. Roch surveyed the shrinking archipelago, he explained how the island began to dissolve:

> What hastened the erosion process was, first of all, when they leveed the Mississippi River. Then, to make it worse, they blocked Bayou Laforche, in Donaldsonville, that connects with the Mississippi River and brings a lot of fresh water to this area, all the way to the Gulf. We used to have real good soil, farming land, and grow all kinds of good vegetables. But then they started exploring for oil in this general area. So marsh buggies would cut through the marshes and make tracks. I mean, they leave like a highway, almost. So they went criss-crossing the marshes and all. There's also a whole mess of pipelines this way, at each end of the island. So they hastened the erosion because they dug those canals. It was like building a new highway. It allowed more traffic to come in and faster. They were not blocked from the current—once the currents get in there, I mean it just started eroding, eating it away.

Fr. Roch noted, painfully, that oil has now been found under the island. Someday, these one hundred homes will be gone, water will cover the land and off-shore oil drilling will begin on what was once the Isle de Jean Charles.

BISCO leaders point to the island as an example of what's in store for the state if coastal erosion remains unchecked. The situation is a bit like the story of the people of Carteret Islands, located near Australia, who must resettle before rising tides finish the job of destroying their homes. Their story is the subject of a documentary film, *Sun Come Up*, widely promoted by the

Catholic Climate Covenant. American audiences have expressed deep concern over the plight of the Carteret Islanders. Have environmental leaders noticed that the same type of eviction-by-climate-change is happening here in the United States? BISCO has.

Scientists have developed some encouraging schemes to slow down the erosion, but one of the most promising ideas has emerged locally. BISCO is now using its clout to draw attention to local retired engineer and tinkerer Webster Pierce. His "Wave Robber" apparatus not only stops erosion—it reverses it!

David Gauthe led the way to Webster Pierce's studio in Cut Off, a boyhood home transformed into an inventor's workshop. David is BISCO director Sharon Gauthe's husband, another leader-turned-organizer from within BISCO's ranks. A friendly, affable Cajun, burly enough to wrestle an alligator (two years ago, inside a convenience store), David emphasizes BISCO's commitment to local solutions. "The people who live down here, they're the ones who know how tides go in and out, as communities. Yet they're never asked their opinion, when it comes to projects. It's always somebody from outside the area that's helping the federal government make the decision, instead of the people who are here."

Webster greeted us with all the excitement of an inventor about to unveil his latest creation. His son, Andrew, who helps his elderly father when not working offshore on oil rigs, joined us. In what used to be his grandparents' living room, Webster had set up a model of the Wave Robber with accompanying charts explaining how the apparatus works. He handed me a small plastic packet of dirt, the Ziploc bag about the size one might store a few screws. Its label read, "New Louisiana Soil: This sediment was reclaimed by the Wave Robber. Patent No. 8,226,325 B1."

The Wave Robber is deceptively simple. It's an eight-foot-wide, five-foot-tall plastic structure with ascending stairs punctured by semicircle holes like cartoon mouse holes. It is designed to be placed right at the shoreline, where waves break. When waves hit the box, they lose kinetic energy and never reach the shore—it's the same principle behind dropping giant rocks in the Gulf: if the waves hit something other than the shoreline, they don't erode it. But what's different about the Wave Robber is what happens next, when a wave hits the "stairs." The water, containing tiny amounts of sediment, enters the "mouseholes" and travels down pipes to the bottom of the Wave Robber. The sediment collects, adding land, surely as a dripping faucet adds up to gallons of water. "I'm mining for sediment," Webster explained. "Like you mine for gold. I'm mining for sediment."

BISCO's promotion of the Wave Robber (training Webster in media relations and helping him connect to small business experts) attracted the attention of the University of Louisiana, which has assigned a graduate student to monitor the Wave Robber prototype. We drove to the experimental model, near the levee in Cut Off, and walked to the site, just at the water's edge. Sure enough, a five-foot-wide, twelve-foot-long peninsula jutted out of the coast where the Wave Robber had stood for eleven months—a testimony to a local engineer who set his mind to one of the great engineering challenges of his times. With BISCO's help, this pilot project may be replicated throughout the Gulf Coast, returning land lost during the twentieth century, several grains of sediment at a time.

"If only we'd had people like Mr. Webster back some thirty or forty years ago, when the Isle de Jean Charles was going strong," David said as we drove away from the levee. "They used to grow cows and wheat, and hunt turkey on the island. Now it's down to twenty-three, twenty-four families. That's it. Everybody else, after being beat up, beat up, beat up, beat up, decided to relocate to another location. Now what's really bad about this is that when you relocate a band of Native American Indians, it makes it difficult to get any kind of federal recognition."

Members of the United Houma Nation like Coy, and other BISCO leaders like Chief Albert Naquin of the Biloxi-Chitimacha-Choctaw Tribe, have state, but not federal, recognition as tribes. If they become dispersed throughout Louisiana and other states, the case for federal recognition will only become weaker. Coastal erosion therefore threatens to wash away peoples as well as land. BISCO's struggle is as much a fight for cultural preservation as it is for preservation of the land. It is without question the greatest challenge the organization has ever faced—healing the earth from the damage done by God's errant stewards.

Beyond Empowerment II

BISCO offers a great example of the dilemmas success in organizing provokes. Their leaders developed enough power to convince the city of Thibodaux to add swimming and recreation programs for children. BISCO forged a strong relationship with law enforcement, impacting policing throughout Terrebonne Parish. It became the leading community spokesperson in the wake of the BP oil disaster. Do they have enough power to take on coastal erosion and climate change, the greatest challenges of all? In some ways, this is the ultimate question—about BISCO and about all organizing projects.

What's at stake is not only land and livelihoods, but also culture. If, as many scientists predict, Louisiana will lose over 1,700 square miles of land over the next 50 years,[5] what will remain of the Native Americans who currently live and work on the bayous and in the wetlands? What would their culture look like, apart from this environment, and if they dispersed, would *any* of it endure? These questions shift BISCO's mission from simply developing power for change to the prevention of cultural genocide.

The organization's weapons are learning the assets of a vulnerable people through the discipline of thousands of 1:1 meetings and then utilizing those talents in a new way. Consider Coy and Miss Eloise becoming spokespersons and advocates, Webster putting his engineering skills to work on community problems, Sharon calming a crowd of angry fishermen to show them how to get what they really want. Along the way, leaders from each of the main racial/ethnic groups that comprise BISCO—Native American, African American, Cajun, and Anglo gain an appreciation of each other's ways of life and a commitment to preserving not only land, but the cultures of Bayou Country.

Cultural preservation is the thread that runs through both of these south Louisiana organizing (BISCO) and economic development (Café Reconcile) projects. Each of the two CCHD-funded groups helps its leaders draw from the best of their cultures, demonstrating that even the "least of these," those excluded from the table of public life, have skills, ideas, perspectives, and dreams to offer. Perhaps no one demonstrates this principle better than the immigrant Latinas of central and western Washington State, to whom we now turn.

Chapter 2

Meet the *Lideresas*: Women's Justice Circles

Doubly poor are those women who endure situations of exclusion, mistreatment and violence, since they are frequently less able to defend their rights. Even so, we constantly witness among them impressive examples of daily heroism in defending and protecting their vulnerable families.

—Pope Francis
The Joy of the Gospel, no. 212

Luz Balderas never planned to immigrate to the United States, let alone raise her children in faraway Washington State. Guanajuato, a small state in central Mexico, would always be home. The historically significant region (producing, at one point, two-thirds of the world's silver), with its narrow streets and alleys, long staircases built into mountainsides, and local foods like *enchiladas mineras*, maintained a strong hold on her heart. But her husband had built a life in Washington, traveling back and forth to the rhythms of the agricultural seasons, like so many other Mexican workers.

"One time when he came back," she recalled, "My four-year-old daughter said, 'Mommy, the man is here.'" In an instant, Luz made the decision. She wanted her children to know their father.

*The Women's Justice Circle prepares for testimony before the
Human Rights Commission.*

When Abel, "the man," next prepared to return to Washington,
she and the children would accompany him. "I didn't want to
happen what's happened to so many families, when the husbands
come over here to the U.S., they make their life here and have
a family here, while the wife and children stay there in Mexico
because they don't have documents," she said.

In 1992, Luz made the trip to Sunnyside, Washington, a
town of sixteen thousand people nestled alongside endless apple
orchards, five children at her side. Her husband was clear about
his expectations. "He told me, 'It's going to be difficult. But
you're going to stay home, and I'm going to work.'" Luz complied.

"I would just focus on my children and my house," she said.
"The only time I left my home was on Saturdays to get grocer-
ies, and then on Sundays we would go to church. Saturday was
the only day we had any kind of excursion for our children.
We'd shop in the town of Granger and go to the park, which is
a common weekend for Mexican women from rural towns and
small communities."

When her children grew up and left home, Luz realized she could step out of the house more often. At church, announcements described programs for women at *Nuestra Casa*, a multiservice center founded and run by Holy Names Sister Mary Rita Rohde. "They were giving aerobics classes," she said. "And I've always wanted to lose weight! I came and really enjoyed it."

But Luz found more than physical fitness at *Nuestra Casa*. The center took a broad approach to the educational needs of Latinas who are low income, typically arriving in Sunnyside with a third-grade education. Luz became acquainted with women taking English as a Second Language (ESL) classes, driver's education, parenting, cooking, and citizenship courses. The atmosphere of learning and growth was exciting, and the new friends enriched her life.

In 2006, Sr. Mary Rita approached Luz about joining a Women's Justice Circle, a group of ten to twelve women who would meet weekly for eight weeks to try to make a difference on the most pressing concerns in their lives. In the process, they would claim both their own power and that generated by collaboration. Along the way, Circle members would learn the skills of grassroots organizing and act to change some larger dimension of their lives. Luz considered the invitation. It sounded like an adventure!

A theme guided each of the eight meetings, beginning with getting acquainted, followed by naming the issues of most concern to group members. Then, by consensus, the Women's Justice Circle selected an issue to address, researched that issue, and took action. Action could mean writing letters, talking to elected or appointed officials, organizing events—whatever the circumstances called for. Every meeting also included an opportunity for each woman to take inventory of her own personal growth and leadership development.

As part of the second session, "In the Company of Powerful Women," Luz and the other eleven participants each inscribed the name of a woman who had been a powerful presence in her life on a wooden heart, placed it in the center of the circle, and then wrote that woman, living or dead, a letter. Luz wrote a letter to Sr. Mary Rita, who guided her development as a leader. Others chose their own mothers or grandmothers. The reading of these letters produced a flow of tears that transformed this group of strangers into a Women's Justice Circle: a circle of protection, power, life, and leadership.

Luz quickly befriended Guadalupe Santana, who had emigrated from the rural districts of Veracruz, Mexico, in the 1990s, for reasons similar to her own. Guadalupe hated the off-and-on separation from her husband Jaime. "I would be alone at home in the town," she said, "and I didn't want to be alone there anymore." After five years, she had had enough. Guadalupe left Veracruz, and made the nearly three-thousand-mile trek to Sunnyside. Like Luz, she became involved in *Nuestra Casa* through its educational offerings. Cooking classes were her favorite. She, like Luz, worked her way up to the 2006 Women's Justice Circle.

When it came time to discuss public issues, Guadalupe first offered concerns about family income, the domestic violence friends and neighbors faced, and the gangs and drugs that shadowed her children. But it was only after she felt more comfortable with the group that she shared the issue that concerned her most—a particularly toxic standardized test used throughout the state's schools: the WASL (Washington Assessment of Student Learning).

Guadalupe's mention of the WASL immediately resonated with Luz. Her eldest daughter—an "A" student—had failed the test and would not graduate from high school. Luz was livid. "How can a child who is getting A's, who has done her homework, who's involved in school, how could she not be graduating?" she asked. "That became a very personal issue for me. It was very difficult to see how one test could do this. And if *she* had good grades, what's going to happen to the rest? And maybe one of those students is going to marry my daughter!" Guadalupe shared her own children's difficulty sleeping the night before the WASL and the stories she heard about children leaving school early because of panic attacks associated with the test. The WASL was not only a threat to her children's educational progress, it endangered their health.

The consensus was clear: this group of marginalized Latinas would take on the Washington State educational establishment and advocate for abolishing the WASL. But where to start? With coaching from facilitator Sr. Grace Diaz, SNJM, group members began to meet with policy makers locally. A sit-down meeting with local school superintendent Dr. Richard Cole affirmed what many suspected: the WASL was a state-mandated test, and local school districts could not opt out. Yet the meeting produced an unexpected outcome, an acknowledgment of power. The women had invited their husbands and a few friends to the meeting; at most they numbered thirty. But Dr. Cole was overheard saying in the days following the meeting, "I met with a hundred immigrant women down in Sunnyside." This statement carried two lessons for the Justice Circle. First, although it was a mixed-gender group, he remembered them as a women's group. This was not their everyday experience. Second, he unconsciously tripled their numbers, suggesting, perhaps, that each had the strength of three!

Attempts to meet with State Superintendent of Public Instruction Terry Bergeson, beginning in December, proved frustrating, as the women met with delay after delay. Finally, Bergeson agreed to travel to Sunnyside at the worst possible time, in May, when most immigrants were tied up harvesting asparagus, and meeting turnout would be low. Eight women, nevertheless, attended, including Luz and Guadalupe.

Superintendent Bergeson explained that the WASL was legally mandated by the Washington legislature. Even if she wanted to, she did not have the power to discontinue the test. That would require a new law.

Luz and Guadalupe's Justice Circle quickly became a laboratory of democracy, their campaign a civics lesson more powerful than any citizenship course could offer. They learned that a new law would need to be introduced as a bill by a state representative or senator. The women invited Rep. Dan Neuhausen (R-Sunnyside) to discuss such a bill.

At first, Neuhausen was noncommittal, even dodgy. Luz took the role of "pinner," the leader who tries to "pin down" an answer, asking him directly, "What are you going to do to get rid of the WASL?" Rep. Neuhausen responded, "I don't really think I can do anything. I wasn't in the legislature when the bill was passed." Luz persisted, pressing him, "No, I know that. What are you going to do *now*?" The third time she asked, he answered, "Well, I do know the minority (party) leader on the education committee in the House of Representatives. How about I have her call?"

As the "Ban the WASL" bill was introduced, with Rep. Neuhausen as sponsor, the Justice Circle approached the local school board for a resolution endorsing the bill. Of the ten local residents attending that month's school board meeting, each was a member of the Justice Circle. The resolution passed unanimously. Meanwhile, in the state capital, Olympia, new allies had discovered the bill.

"Everyone hated the WASL," explained J. L. Drouhard, Archdiocese of Seattle CCHD director. "There was widespread dissatisfaction with the test across the state among both parents and teachers. You'd hear a lot of complaining, but this group in Sunnyside did something about it." Teachers, parents, even school administrators previously supportive of the test piled on. Both Republican and Democratic legislators cosponsored the bill; it passed in 2008, and schools administered the WASL for the last time in the spring of 2009. Today, standardized testing like the Measurements of Student Progress (MSP) and the High School Proficiency Exam (HSPE) takes up a much smaller fraction of the school year, and results are used as just one measure of student progress.

The achievement thrilled Luz and Guadalupe. Within the Circle they had developed new skills, deepened relationships, and even altered the course of education reform in Washington State! Luz went on to cofacilitate a second Women's Justice

Circle at *Nuestra Casa.* This Circle fought successfully to reverse Great Recession cutbacks threatening a Sunnyside community center. She has since served on fourteen local nonprofit boards of directors and as a parent representative to the state Board of Education. Where she once was, as Sr. Mary Rita described, "a quiet housewife who didn't participate in community life," she now thrives as a community leader.

Guadalupe took a different path, becoming a local business leader and introducing Jaime and their son Hector to community action. She reflected on the impact of the Women's Justice Circle on her own growth as a leader. "I developed because it gave me a sense of security," she said, "With that sense of security, I became a citizen. And because of that sense of security, I was able to get a license to run a day care center. And it was also important to me that my son and my husband also became involved, serving on the school board advisory council."

Justice Circle members widely shared this sense of personal security and power in interviews throughout Washington State, where they are primarily seeded. Once lingering in the shadows, they now step forward. United and empowered by their experience of reforming standardized testing, Circle members now take on many of the other challenges facing low-income immigrant women in Washington State.

The Challenge:
Poverty, Family Violence, and Life in the Shadows

Latinas of the Justice Circles face many challenges. Some are migrant farm workers, paid less than minimum wage, choking on pesticides in the apple orchards near Sunnyside. Others are homeless, or recently incarcerated, fruitlessly seeking affordable housing in the booming Seattle economy and stigmatized by their prison records. A large percentage are victims of domestic violence, abuse sanctioned by a *machista* culture permeating parts of the Hispanic Latino community. Almost all work in low-wage sectors, dogged by wage theft and a cycle of poverty offering few ways out.

In Washington State, Hispanic Latino poverty stands at 26.1 percent, compared to 12.9 percent for all residents. A third of all Hispanic Latino high school students drop out without graduating, while 19.6 percent of whites do not complete secondary studies.[1] Fully 15.3 percent of Hispanic Latinos in Washington State are unemployed, while the unemployment rate for whites stands at 8.5 percent.[2]

Precise figures on the incidence of domestic violence within Washington's Latino communities are not available, but the women participating in the Justice Circles identify it as a continuing concern. Exacerbating the problem is the lack of bilingual professionals in law enforcement and services for battered women. The fear of deportation or having their children removed also keeps many women from seeking help.

In interview after interview, women shared stories of sluggish or nonexistent responses to 911 calls, poor road upkeep, a bridge closed for years awaiting repairs that never came, cutbacks in health services essential to children, stroller policies that made it impossible to navigate Olympia's bus system, and other problems—a litany of government neglect.

These challenges loom large for Washington's Latinas, but augmenting each problem is a silence permeating Latino communities, a quietude fostered by cultural norms limiting the role of women in public spaces and the pervasive fear of deportation that characterizes the life of the unauthorized migrant. Living in the shadows, what hope is there of speaking out and making your voice heard, when you're an uneducated woman from rural Mexico, speaking in a language you've only recently adopted? Undocumented Latinas face what sociologists call an "intersectionality" of isms—sexism, racism, classism, and so on—interacting and amplifying their effects.

They may face an array of disempowering structures, and sometimes get discouraged, but there is something to be admired about women who possess enough grit and determination to make it to the United States, learn English, navigate the various new systems, raise children fluent in two languages and cultures, and then cook dinner for everyone. Such women must possess inner resources worth cultivating.

So thought Sr. Linda Haydock, SNJM, who explained how Seattle's Intercommunity Peace & Justice Center (IPJC) founded the Women's Justice Circles. "Among the founders, all but one of whom were women religious, there had always been a concern for how they could be animators, to educate and form women to be leaders, take their rightful place in society, and be people who can transform our world," she said. The sisters of IPJC researched how they might "accompany" women in the church and on the margins.

Accompanying women in need was nothing new to women religious in the United States. Their commitments to women living in poverty date back to 1727, when Ursuline sisters sailed up the Mississippi River to minister to prostitutes in what is now the Ninth Ward of New Orleans. But IPJC needed to create a vehicle for the twenty-first century. Three questions guided their leadership:

1. Where was the need?
2. Who was excluded?
3. How can we make a difference?

Each meeting revealed more information; each piece of the discernment process yielded more clarity. As the sisters narrowed their focus to the needs of undocumented Latinas, they discovered that this group had slipped through the cracks of most organizing projects—they were excluded even from efforts to build power for "the excluded"!

Finally, IPJC leaders agreed to develop a new model of organizing that would, as Sr. Linda put it, "honor women's way of knowing and help them find their voice," in a manner that would "help them go to the next level of organizing on a larger scale among multiple groups: from unions to churches, to community organizations, etc." That new model, the Women's Justice Circle, would begin with eight weekly meetings to prepare people to bring their voice into the public arena. As noted earlier, each session focuses on a different dimension of public life, leading to some form of action in the public arena. Ritual sharing abounds but always for the sake of social change.

Organizers convened each Circle within a different institutional context. Originally, groups were located in different ministries sponsored by religious communities: transitional housing, multiservice centers like *Nuestra Casa*, services-enriched housing, recovery programs for women, domestic violence programs—each a different social services venue. Today, the variety of contexts is even broader, including a group of prison inmates, residents of prerelease homes, parents of children with intellectual and developmental disabilities, and a Latina mothers' support group, for example—wherever women on the margins come together.

The first group convened in 2000 and conducted meetings in English. Today, in Washington State, over fifteen groups meet per year. Seventy percent converse in Spanish at the meetings; most of the rest are run in English. Giselle Cárcamo coordinates Women's Justice Circles and has facilitated several Circles. She describes one of the hardest dimensions of running a group as making sure the women don't come to see others as the source of their newfound power. "Sometimes they think someone else is giving them power," she said. "And I'm like, 'No—wait a minute. Your power comes from within. Trust the process!'"

Trusting the process is not always easy, Giselle explained. "There was a Circle that was having a lot of difficulties. It was a group of women in a transitional living situation run by one of our partnering ministries. They hoped to provide the women with community organizing skills and an opportunity for empowerment. Unlike the typical Justice Circle, participation was a program requirement," she said. "The turning point came when they discussed why they didn't want to do it. They said they didn't even know what social justice was—so many issues affected them. But one of them said, 'You know what, I'm an ex-felon. I feel like I carry an 'X' on me and no matter what I do, how I behave, or how many classes I take, I continue to be an ex-felon. For me, it's like the 'X' is fluorescent!'"

The modern-day image of a fluorescent "Scarlet Letter" resonated with the residents of Sojourner Place, a "refuge for women committed to working on the causes of their homelessness." One by one, they began to disclose, "I'm an ex-felon too!" and what Giselle calls a "chain of truth" emerged. Now energized, they decided to focus on access to housing and jobs for people with felony records. They testified before the Seattle Human Rights Commission sharing their stories and desire to (1) reunite with their families, (2) get a second chance in life, (3) improve their chances of finding decent housing and securing employment. Commission members spoke to city councilors. Three years later, the city council passed a "Jobs Assistance Ordinance" including a nondiscrimination clause regarding ex-inmates and acknowledged the women of Sojourner Place in the press release announcing the change.

Since their inception, two hundred Circles have been organized in more than forty-five cities and towns. Many have enrolled in a recently developed advanced training program while others have simply continued to meet to work for change. Giselle explained that the victories are important in the way they change society, but also key is how "their victory enriches women's self-esteem and increases their civic engagement." Each Women's Justice Circle interlocks with the others, forming a powerful chain of newly empowered women. Within that chain, every Justice Circle operates as a circle of leadership, a circle of protection, a circle of life, and a circle of power.

A Circle of Leadership

Alma Meza learned about Women's Justice Circles through her ten-year-old daughter Wendy's afterschool program, New Futures. Her subsidized apartment building in the city of Burien, Washington, offers New Futures to resident children without charge. The New Futures Justice Circle recruited mothers of the children enrolled in the afterschool program. Alma and her husband both work, he as a sushi chef and she as a home health aide, but they still live paycheck-to-paycheck, without much in the way of assets.

Alma enjoyed getting to know her neighbors in the Circle. Previously, most had never spoken to her (or each other), even though their children often played together. The first session of the 2013 group, she recalled, had been awkward. "Nobody wanted to talk; nobody was sharing. We were all like, 'Who are you?'"

But, she explained, the group began to bond when they described the issues that most upset them.

> The person leading the group asked what were some of the things that bothered people in the community. The first person said she was concerned about not knowing exactly where her child would be during the afterschool program. The second person said, "I'm worried about the safety of my child going from the school to the apartment." We were all like, "Yeah! That's a huge deal!" Everything else we thought of was secondary to that issue. It was something we could work on.

A short walking path connected the front door of their apartment building to Military Road, where Hilltop Elementary School stood, just across the street. But time had worn the crosswalk bare, and the city of Burien, bordering Seattle, had never repainted it. Military Road arcs just before the school, so cars whip around the blind curve at high speeds. With no crosswalk and no crossing guards, kids are on their own.

I asked Wendy if she felt safe crossing. "No!" she cried, "You try to cross and you're just like waiting, and the cars don't stop!" Occasionally, an angry-enough-to-stop-traffic mom would jump into the street and assume the role of crossing guard, but this desperate move often resulted in near collisions as cars, not even braking, would swerve to avoid striking her.

Meetings with the Hilltop Elementary principal and PTA leaders yielded a commitment to raising money for parent crossing guard uniforms while they pressed their case with the city. Letters to the city council then sparked an investigation. After two months, a city engineer reported the traffic data: 15 percent of drivers sped through the invisible crosswalk at thirty-seven miles per hour during school hours, when the speed limit was twenty miles per hour. He noted (writing on New Year's Eve, 2013) that in 2014 the city of Burien would assign a uniformed crossing guard and "restripe the existing crosswalk, install two reflective markers in front of each ladder stripe on the approach side of the crosswalk, and install advance warning signs" as well as seek grant funding for "Rectangular Rapid Flash Beacons (RRFB)."

Within a year's time the group had won a significant victory on the crosswalk safety issue, ignored for so long by the city. Even more important, the group members' confidence and sense of personal capability soared. Here were residents of subsidized housing, who averted their gaze whenever a neighbor approached. Yet, after weeks of leadership development, they spoke up, made themselves heard, and achieved concrete results. At the same time they built community within the building.

Alma spoke of her own growth, "I know now that if I need to do something, I can do it if I put myself into it. Nothing is going to change if I get it into my head that I can't do it. So if I do have an issue now, I address it with confidence." Looking back, she echoed the organizing maxim, "The issue isn't the issue; it's the person," explaining, "It wasn't just the crosswalk, it was everything else. We talked about if you suffer any kind of violence, any kind of abuse, you can get over that. There were people in the group who had gone through family violence. That wasn't supposed to be the main focus, but that's what was shared. It was very open. You could get over whatever was making you feel lower than anyone else."

Alma's newfound confidence spilled over into her work life. Recently, a client's father called to complain about her performance providing care for his daughter. In the past, she said, she would have thought, "If they think I'm wrong, I'm probably wrong." But this time she noted her devotion to the mother's instructions for the care of her daughter. The man's conflict was with his wife—not Alma—she reasoned. "So I defended myself," she explained. "We went to the office, to my boss. I wrote up everything I did that day and the instructions I was given, and my boss said I was right. I was able to defend myself."

Alma continues to flourish at work, Wendy excels at school, and the Circle continues to meet, keeping on top of the crosswalk upgrade. Alma takes pride in her contribution but eschews the word "leader." "I don't feel comfortable being a leader," she said. I protested, "But didn't you get the crosswalk taken care of?" She answered, "Yes, but it wasn't just me, it was the whole group. I would call that teamwork."

Later, I asked Giselle, who supervises each Circle, why Alma did not consider herself a leader, despite demonstrating many leadership qualities. Indeed, she had been selected for an interview with me because of her leadership in the Circle. Giselle's answer surprised me, sending both of us down a linguistic rabbit hole.

Spanish, Giselle explained, is a gendered language. A Spanish word for leader, *líder*, is typically used in its masculine form. "And when the masculine form is used, people react like we are referring to an authoritarian man," she said.

"Which explains Alma's reaction to being called a leader!" I responded. Giselle offered the feminine form, *lideresa*, as an alternative. "When I say *lideresa*, I'm opening the term to your abilities as a woman, opening you to the possibilities of a woman being a leader," she explained. *Lideresas* operate more cooperatively, listen more carefully, care for group members more attentively—not the dictatorial leadership model associated with *líder*. They produce the "teamwork" Alma identified. Each Justice Circle, as a circle of leaders, would not therefore be accurately described as a *círculo de líderes* but a *círculo de lideresas*, not simply because they are women, but because they have developed an authentic new form of Latina leadership, one of Sr. Linda's original aims.

Could this be the style of leadership Jesus wished for his Apostles? When James and John (and their mother) make a move for a promotion in Matthew's Gospel (20:20-24), and the other Apostles "become indignant," Jesus intervened. He counseled, "[W]hoever wishes to be great among you shall be your servant; whoever wishes to be first among you shall be your slave" (Matt. 20:26-27).

Later, on the eve of his Passion, prior to the Last Supper, Jesus took off his outer garments, wrapped a towel around his waist, and proceeded to wash the feet of the Apostles (John 13). Afterwards, he explained, "You call me 'teacher' and 'master,' and rightly so, for indeed I am. If I, therefore, the master and teacher, have washed your feet, you ought to wash one another's feet. I have given you a model to follow, so that as I have done for you, you should also do" (John 13:13-15). The Women's Justice Circles of leadership capture the spirit of Jesus's servant leadership in a twenty-first-century context, developing the *lideresa*.

A Circle of Protection

When Lupita Zamora arrived in the United States in 2002, she came with a mission: to help people from her home state of Guanajuato, Mexico, flourish in their new country. Unlike many of the women involved in the Justice Circles, Lupita had grown up watching her mother and beloved *abuela* take leadership in several community organizations. Her family instilled in her "a passion for justice," and she, in turn, sought to help women "build their self-esteem and exercise their power," just like the strong women she admired.

Lupita worked in various human services for years, in Texas and Washington State, and became acquainted with the Women's Justice Circles as a participant in a Circle at St. Mary's Church, Seattle. After a year, Lupita became a cofacilitator. In 2012, she teamed up with Patty Repikoff, coordinator of the Eastside Catholic Community Hispanic Ministry, to lead a Circle of mothers enrolled in parenting classes at St. Brendan Catholic Church in Bothell. Such classes also served also as domestic violence prevention classes, adopting a neutral title like "parenting class." "At first, they had their heads down in shame and fear," Patty recalled.

"The parenting class helped them regain confidence and develop bonds of support."

The class also helped uncover the issue that the Bothell Washington Circle would ultimately take on—their young children were being bullied at school. Bullying affects more than one in four children in Washington State with sixth graders (32 percent) victimized most, among middle and high school students.[3] The women I spoke to insisted that undocumented migrants face a higher than average share of bullying. Mothers involved in the Women's Justice Circle interviewed their children and their children's friends to better understand the bullying and the contexts in which it occurred.

Circle participants, in consultation with experts, then created a Spanish brochure on bullying to offer parents information about the signs and symptoms as well as concrete tips for discussions with children. The brochure was the first outreach material on bullying in Spanish to be introduced in Washington State. It is now widely used by school districts and social work agencies.

The Bothell Circle also hosted the first bullying prevention forum to be held in Spanish in Washington State, for the Northshore School District. They gathered sixty parents, thirty children, and a host of community experts and school personnel for workshops, panels, and an art show developed by the children of Justice Circle members. Volunteer leaders demonstrated how to use storytelling to teach effective responses to bullies. Soon afterwards, another school district and a Catholic parish, as well as two Bothell elementary schools, invited the Circle to lead similar events in Spanish, which the group happily organized.

Looking back on the experience, Patty was most taken with watching the women reclaim their own power: "One person, Maru, said, 'I've been called all kinds of names—illegal, alien, dog, and these are the ones I can tell you—but I know in God's eyes I'm beloved. You can call me anything you want, but I know who I am.'" For Patty, it was as if the group had been looking at the world through a narrow lens, but the Justice Circle then offered a wider way of seeing the world, providing the tools of public life in the context of confidential support, prayer, study, and action.

Patty described the Women's Justice Circles as the "modern-day Christian Family Movement," akin to the small groups of Catholic parents who, from the late 1940s on (reaching a peak of fifty thousand U.S. families in 1964) utilized the "See-Judge-Act" model to better understand and act upon their faith amidst the challenges of modern life. But, she added, "We include 'Celebrate!' after 'Act!'"

The comparisons to the Christian Family Movement may transcend methodology. Some of the husbands recently asked, "Hey, what about us?" observing their wives' leadership development. Giselle responded that a pilot Parents' Justice Circle may be in the works, but care would need to be taken (like training men and women separately) to ensure that the women don't fade into the background to let the men run the group.

Campaigns like the Bothell Circle's antibullying effort under-score the need for at least some women-only groups. Is it a great surprise that women in a domestic violence prevention–focused parenting group would select bullying as an issue? No doubt, many have seen it in their own lives. Would they have selected this issue in a mixed group with their husbands?

As women facing the common challenges of parenthood and perhaps domestic violence and other forms of bullying, the Both-ell Justice Circle became a kind of "circle of protection" for the women participating. Perhaps if they had had such a protective circle in the past, they would not have been bullied, whether by spouses or others in their lives. But now they offer a circle of protection to the wider community in addition to their own children, connected in solidarity with all who need help to stand up to bullies.

A Circle of Life

Jaqueline García formed the *Círculo de Mamás Conscientes* in 2010 to gather Mexican women in the Seattle area to renew their ancestral methods of raising children. Like so many others, she had followed her husband, Fernando, who came to Seattle seeking work four years earlier, ultimately becoming a U.S. citizen along with her husband. Alone in a strange country, she formed the mothers' group as a way of meeting new people and maintaining Mexican culture.

A respected dentist in Mexico, Jaqueline found her credentials worthless in the United States. She faced a choice: return to school and study to become recertified in dentistry or double down on her dream of developing a support network for Latina mothers. She chose the latter, lowering family income substantially, but, she said, "When my son arrived into my life, he changed *everything* that I thought before. And motherhood made me feel equally passionate about social justice, especially what relates to immigrant moms, just like myself. I discovered I no longer cared that much about my career, but instead, I wanted to help women—to help women become *leaders*."

After a year of supportive discussions on child-rearing, Jaqueline looked for a way to take her group to a new level of leadership. She explained, "I took my baby to the clinic and saw a flyer for workshops for Latina leaders who might lead Women's Justice Circles. I was drawn to it because I felt like I could identify with what the flyer was saying. I was a Latina; I was a leader—I had already started my organization of moms!"

Jaqueline led the group through the initial sessions. As the women became more comfortable with each other, one of the participants, Miranda (pseudonym), shared a serious concern. In the wake of an unexpected pregnancy, she was considering having an abortion. As a single mother, Miranda was not sure if she wanted to have another child. The challenges she anticipated were overwhelming. Tears flowed as she offered her story and conflicted feelings to the group. A calm fell over the Circle as each member communicated words of support and comfort.

With a focus on motherhood, Circle members began to unpack the obstacles to successful child-rearing in the United States. One group member shared her experience of being let go from a job after she gave birth. No explanation, no offer to return after a few months; she was essentially fired for having a baby. As they discussed the interconnected issues of discrimination against pregnant women and inadequate maternity leave, the Circle discovered a pattern: many Latinas do not know their rights, and the benefits to which they are entitled are not enough. The Family Leave Act (which provides up to twelve weeks of unpaid leave for employees of organizations with fifty or more employees) was virtually unknown to the group. Even after they studied the provisions of the act, the women were unimpressed—taking unpaid leave was not feasible for families living in poverty. "As one of the great powers of the world and as a country whose babies are the future, they should treasure those babies more," Jaqueline noted.

Group members began to plan legislative advocacy on the state and municipal level to expand access to maternity leave—preferably paid. Though their activities on this issue have not yet yielded policy change, Circle members were overjoyed to learn they had an impact on Miranda's decision regarding her baby. With the support of the Circle, Miranda spent weeks discerning the right action to take on her pregnancy and ultimately surprised herself. She *did* have the strength to bring her baby boy to term. Miranda contemplated abortion for a time, because her poverty and lack of employment might mean she would not be able to handle the challenges of pregnancy. But with a community of support from the Justice Circle, she brought new life into the world and put her baby up for adoption.

Even without yet changing public policy on maternity leave, the group's solidarity had saved a life. A baby boy would be born, and a family eager to adopt would raise him. This Circle, like so many others, could be understood as a Circle of life as well as a Circle of justice. If their solidarity and support had saved one baby's life, how many more would be saved if women did not have to worry about losing their jobs for being pregnant? How many women would choose to keep their babies if the United States offered maternity benefits comparable to those of other industrialized nations? In a country where over a million abortions take place annually, such policy changes would certainly reduce the burdens and sense of desperation that drive some women to elect to have abortions.

When asked what aspect of the Women's Justice Circles she was most proud of, Jaqueline replied, "The moment when women actually realize that they have power in themselves to create change." Group facilitator after group facilitator reported the same. It is a "eureka" moment, and the world never looks the same again after a woman owns "the ability to act" that was always there. But as Giselle noted earlier, it is the Women's Justice Circle *process* itself that empowers, not the facilitator.

A Circle of Power

As the Women's Justice Circles lead individuals to own and act on their power, each Circle itself becomes a Circle of power. Certainly, individuals like Luz, Guadalupe, Alma, Lupita, Jaqueline, and Miranda came to know and appreciate their own ability to act in public life, but it was only *with others* in the Circle that they developed the power to create change on the issues most important to them. Consider Superintendent Cole's reaction to the *Nuestra Casa* Justice Circle. Overnight, thirty women and men became "one hundred immigrant women." The group radiated power. But imagine Luz meeting with Dr. Cole alone. Regardless of how "empowered" she was, would he have left with the same impression? Not likely.

The secret to the power of the Women's Justice Circles is the power of organized people. When members feel the power of the group, they connect to their own power. This experience is riveting, exciting, life changing. In a society that prizes the "great man" or "great woman" approach to history, we too often neglect the role of groups in changing history. We honor Rosa Parks, but forget she was the secretary of the Montgomery, Alabama, NAACP chapter, which organized the bus boycott. We devote a holiday to Rev. Dr. Martin Luther King, Jr., but we don't even know the names of those blasted by Sheriff Bull Connor's fire hoses. The Women's Justice Circles operate on the individual and group levels, developing groups powerful enough to change social structures in several areas of life, while still empowering individual women.

In 2013, one Circle of domestic violence survivors took on the issue of inhumane conditions at the Northwest Detention Center (NWDC), a privately owned prison in Tacoma, after a Circle member told her story of being forced to strip in front of a male guard. The NWDC is the facility where survivors of torture, domestic violence, sexual abuse, and human trafficking are held, in addition to other detained immigrants, while their applications for asylum are heard. The result of illegal actions like the strip search is a retraumatization of people who have come to the United States to escape violations of human dignity.

The Circle produced a brochure in Spanish providing information to immigrants about their legal rights, including tips on how to respond to immigration agents at work, home, or in public. Members also joined the NWDC Roundtable, an advocacy group working on behalf of detainees housed in the NWDC, and spoke to local officials about holding GEO Group Corporation, the company that runs the facility, accountable to human rights standards. That dialogue also led to contributions from the City of Seattle Latino Employees organization to help domestic violence survivors held in the NWDC.

Another Circle started in an unusual venue: Purdy, the Washington State Corrections Center for Women, bringing together women involved with Girl Scouts Beyond Bars (a national program developed to equip girls aged 5 to 17 whose mothers are incarcerated with the tools they'll need to succeed and to strengthen the mother-daughter bond through regular visits). These incarcerated women identified "significant debt, the stigma of incarceration, limited education, and employers and communities barring them from employment and housing" as the most significant obstacles they faced in trying to break the cycle of recidivism, intergenerational poverty, and homelessness. As their public action, this Circle chose to advocate for a city of Seattle ordinance banning housing discrimination against formerly incarcerated people convicted of nonviolent, nonsexual offenses. The campaign is still in progress, but thus far, women of the Purdy Circle have provided testimonies and letters to the Seattle City Council, as well as housing providers, in attempts to facilitate successful family reunification.

It is the versatility and nimble qualities of the Women's Justice Circles that created a demand for Circles outside Washington State. First, requests from Latin American countries came in. Giselle was happy to oblige, providing training via Skype until local leaders could take over. She found these groups more challenging to organize because materials needed to be adapted to foreign realities. Still, the training and formation process opened hearts and minds, and participants came to own their own power, acting together. In a Lima, Peru, shantytown, a Circle successfully advocated for more public green spaces. In rural Nicaragua, they worked on a health program to prevent tropical disease; in Bolivia, they organized against gender-based violence; and in the El Salvador countryside, Circle members worked to obtain land titles to prevent railroad expansion from swallowing up their land.

In 2014, Women's Justice Circles expanded to New Brunswick, New Jersey, in the Diocese of Metuchen, where Latinas at two worship sites within Holy Family Parish gathered. As the Women's Justice Circles model becomes more widely known, additional groups throughout the United States will likely follow. Traditional congregation-based organizing projects like BISCO (Chapter 1) and its many cousins in the national networks can't help but miss organizing some who would benefit from the power of a mediating institution. Low-income Latinas, particularly, seem to slip through the cracks. But beneath those cracks, throughout Washington State, are circles of leadership, protection, life, and power to catch them. Once trained, connected, and empowered, these Circles can take on the more challenging job of fixing the cracks, what the Hebrew tradition calls *Tikkun olam*, or "repair of the world."

Beyond Empowerment

The Women's Justice Circles have given hundreds of Latinas the ability to act in public life for the first time. Most of these women, like Alma and Luz, use that power to improve their personal lives as well. "Empowerment" is an integral part of the Circles and the language its members use to describe the experience.

J. L. Drouhard, CCHD director for the Archdiocese of Seattle, has seen the effects of this empowerment. "On our annual legislative advocacy day in Olympia, we used to draw together a couple hundred white middle-class retired people who could afford to take a day off," he explained. "Visibly, the women of the Justice Circles are with us now in large numbers, and inspire the rest of us—we bring together over five hundred people now. They help us grow commitment to circles of protection, whether for nutrition, wages, farmworkers, and more."

But J. L., like others who have observed the growth of people like Luz and Alma, believes the Justice Circles offer far more than empowerment—they foster the full flourishing of the human person. He offered a biblical image:

> The Women's Justice Circles are like what Jesus described when he said, "How I wish, like a mother hen, I could gather them together" (Matt. 23:37). I grew up on a farm, and the chicks don't come in a line. They're in a circle under the hen. When the hen puts out its feathers, those chicks are in a circle, in that protection. Our paintings of the Last Supper are of a long table with the Apostles sitting in a line looking out at the painter. But it had to have been a circle, a circle of protection.

J. L. noted that like the Apostles, the Women's Justice Circles begin facing inward, but then shift to an outward stance, still supportive of one another, but engaging the world.

Today's table of public life grows with their participation. "When you meet these women," he added, "when you talk to them, your heart gets enlarged. Then you realize that we're also enlarging our community, enlarging that table. They are helping to do that; their contribution is to expand what we mean by the Good News." The Women's Justice Circles thereby remind us that helping a person living in poverty respond to the call to participation in public life is as much of an imperative of Catholic social teaching as responding to their material needs. For low-wage workers throughout the United States, workers centers have become the vehicle for such participation in the public arena. To learn more, we travel south to Houston, Texas, where we make the first of several stops on our pilgrimage to meet workers in solidarity, fighting wage theft and other threats to human dignity.

Chapter 3

Voices of Solidarity: Workers Centers and Social Enterprises

Wage Theft

A just wage enables [workers] to have adequate access to all the other goods which are destined for our common use.

—Pope Francis
The Joy of the Gospel, no. 192

Zenaida Garcia stared at the rim of the toilet and began scrubbing. Back-and-forth, up-and-down—this was a tough stain. As she rhythmically scoured the bowl, Zenaida's mind wandered to Mexico and her four children living with relatives. Utilizing the $200–400 per month she remitted home for eight years, each had enrolled in a local university. Two studied computer systems, one radiology, the fourth tourism. Zenaida cleaned houses so her children wouldn't have to. Their dreams were her dreams.

"It's payday!" interrupted Griselda, her cleaning partner. Zenaida stood up and examined her paycheck. She cleaned seven houses per day for Spic and Span Cleaners in some of Houston's wealthiest neighborhoods. Her daily wage totaled $40. That was the arrangement she and the other workers made with Esmeralda, the company's owner. But the workdays typically stretched

*LeRoy Graham of Centro de Trabajadores Unidos en Lucha
is arrested at Target headquarters.*

to twelve, even fourteen hours. Her team of four domestic workers found it difficult to clean a home in forty-five minutes and
then virtually teleport to the next house, miles away. If a customer complained, the team would have to return and clean
the house from top to bottom a second time, making for a long
workday.

Zenaida calculated the hourly wage. At best it was $3.33. And
that was before the deduction for transportation between houses,
which totaled $25 weekly. "We're making just over three dollars
an hour," she said. "Can Esmeralda do that?"

"I don't know," Griselda responded, "but I told my friend
about how we are paid, and he said, 'You know what, your boss

can't do that, and you don't have to be silent. You have to go to this place, the *Fe y Justicia* Worker Center. They can help you fight for your rights!'" Together, with a co-worker, Miriam, the three women took a bus to the church housing *Fe y Justicia*'s offices. Zenaida paused and glanced at the posters covering the walls of the office as they entered. "All Religions Believe in Justice," "Thou Shalt Not Steal," "Down with Wage Theft." "Wage theft?" she thought, "What was that?"

After a brief conversation with Executive Director Laura Perez Boston, Zenaida realized that wage theft—employers stealing pay to which employees are legally entitled—was precisely the reason she and her colleagues sat in the *Fe y Justicia* conference room. Their average hourly wage of $3.33/hour totaled less than half of the Texas minimum wage ($7.25/hour). Of the sixty hours she worked that week, twenty should have been paid as overtime, and the transportation charges were illegal. Zenaida had been robbed—by her employer.

The three domestic workers sat down with Laura and reviewed their options. Wage theft was illegal, but Texas limited a victim's legal options. Many workers ultimately settled for much less than what they were owed. Some received nothing when businesses went bankrupt. Even the worst offenders never faced jail time or even fines.

Zenaida, Griselda, and Miriam decided to file a small claims court lawsuit, enlisting fellow workers as coplaintiffs. They would spend many hours organizing reluctant colleagues, who feared deportation. When Zenaida invited another domestic worker to a meeting at *Fe y Justicia*, she responded, "Better watch out; she'll call Immigration!" Whenever Zenaida herself faltered, she remembered one of Esmerelda's tirades: "You guys are undocumented. You come here to clean. And you come here to clean the *mierda*!" She felt a familiar flush of anger. "Yes," she thought. "I am undocumented. But that didn't give you the right to steal our wages."

The Spic and Span workers' missing wages totaled tens of thousands of dollars. Claims went back as far as six years. But the Texas statute of limitations for wage theft allowed only those earnings stolen within three years of the lawsuit's filing date to be retrieved. And a significant number of workers had moved after quitting the company—to where, no one knew. Some would not sign on, simply for fear of Esmerelda. She spoke often of her mother, who served as a police officer in Mexico, to intimidate employees. Would Esmerelda harm their families? To these workers, she was someone you didn't want to cross.

Zenaida and other *Fe y Justicia* leaders organized current and former Spic and Span workers for three and a half years. During that time, allies among the Houston clergy wrote letters urging Esmerelda to pay what she owed, and worker center staff kept the pressure on, organizing worker vigils at Spic and Span headquarters. Finally, Esmerelda settled. Without admitting wrongdoing, she agreed to pay about half of what she owed, an average settlement for a wage theft case. Zenaida responded philosophically: "It is better to have a bird in the hand than a thousand out there flying. And she's going to be thinking about me every month when she pays us." She would eventually receive $3,700.

Texas law prohibits wage theft, but its statutes are written in ways that help employers escape full justice. As noted above, for purposes of the small claims lawsuits, the three-year clock starts from *the moment the worker joins a lawsuit*. One domestic worker, Fanning, joined the lawsuit three years after she quit working for Spic and Span, unaware of this technicality. When the settlement was reached, she learned she would receive nothing. Noting that Fanning had been working on the case eight to ten hours a day at times, tracking down former colleagues on Facebook, Zenaida organized workers who received awards to donate a percentage to her, an expression of the worker solidarity underlying the entire effort.

In 2012, just two months after winning the settlement, Zenaida ran into her cousin, who worked at a salon frequented by Esmerelda. The cousin relayed Esmerelda's caustic parting remark after a recent highlight session: "You know what, your cousin won her lawsuit," she said. "But what I'm happy about is that the lawyer got most of the money."

Zenaida paused at this memory, appearing hurt. Then her passion returned. "What she said is not true. But it's not about just that, it's about justice," she said. "Because we taught our employer that even though we don't have legal status, we do have rights."

The Challenge:
Wage Theft, Poverty Wages, and an
Unsafe Factory Food System

Zenaida is not the only worker whose employer steals wages— she is one victim in a growing epidemic of wage-theft against low-wage workers in the United States and one of the main reasons for the growth of workers centers. Employers steal workers' wages in varied ways. Minimum wage and time-and-a-half overtime laws are frequently ignored, with few consequences for offending employers like Esmerelda. Workers are often improperly misclassified as "exempt" from overtime regulations. Many are inappropriately classified as contractors. An alarming number of employers steal workers' tips, and many do not pay the tipped worker minimum wage. A high number of low-wage workers do not get paid for all of the hours they work, and some do not get paid, period. All told, the volume of wage theft suggests the nation is retreating from the commitments made to American workers during the Progressive Era and the New Deal.

Unauthorized migrants are the hardest hit. Like Zenaida, they are especially vulnerable because of their lack of documentation and tend to be afraid to report abuses to law-enforcement authorities. Many unauthorized migrants, like the domestic workers of Spic and Span, come to the United States out of desperation, aiming to support families living in poverty with the cash remittances they send home.

In September 2009, a nationally recognized team of scholars working on behalf of three research organizations (Center for

Urban Economic Development, University of Illinois at Chicago;
National Employment Law Project [NELP]; UCLA Institute for
Research on Labor and Employment) released the largest study
ever undertaken on wage theft. Over 4,300 low-wage workers
were interviewed in 13 languages by 62 field staff, throughout
New York City, Chicago, and Los Angeles.[1] In all, unauthorized
migrants made up 38.8 percent of workers interviewed,[2] a representative sample of the urban low-wage workforce.

The study revealed widespread and systematic wage violations across many sectors of the low-wage urban economy.
The researchers found that among unauthorized immigrants
interviewed

- 37.1 percent experienced minimum wage violations in
  the week prior to the study. The rate for men was 29.5
  percent; the rate for women was 47.4 percent.[3]
- 84.9 percent experienced overtime violations in the week
  prior to the study. The sex of workers did not make a
  significant difference in the rate of overtime violations.[4]
- 76.3 percent experienced "off the clock" violations in the
  week prior to the study, meaning they were not paid for
  some of the work they performed during the previous
  week.[5]

The widespread incidence of wage theft was not limited to
unauthorized immigrants. Among authorized immigrants, 21.3
percent experienced minimum wage violations, 67.2 percent
were the victims of overtime violations, and 68.9 percent faced
"off the clock" violations, all within the week prior to the study.
For U.S.-born low-wage workers, the rates were smaller, but still
appalling: 15.6 percent experienced minimum wage violations,
68.2 percent reported not being paid for overtime, and 67.0
percent reported "off the clock" violations.[6] The average worker
lost $51 per week, receiving $329 instead of the $380 they truly
earned. This level of wage theft translates to $2,634 annually, 15
percent of true annual earnings of $17,616.[7]

What would you do with a 15 percent raise? How would a person living in poverty utilize a windfall like that? Consider the impact on the economy if wage theft disappeared overnight.

When Zenaida's friend said, "Better watch out—she'll call Immigration!" she gave voice to a common fear among unauthorized immigrant workers. The 2009 study found high percentages of employer retaliation against workers who complained of wage theft. Among workers who made complaints, 62.1 percent experienced one or more forms of illegal retaliation. The most common forms of retaliation were threatening to call immigration authorities, firing or suspending workers, and cutting workers' hours or pay.[8] Among those who did not step forward with complaints, 20 percent said they held back because of fears of such retaliation.[9]

How can it be that basic worker protection laws are so flagrantly violated? Isn't the government supposed to enforce these laws? The U.S. Government Accountability Office (GAO) looked into this question from July 2008 to March 2009, investigating complaints about the Wage and Hour Division (WHD) of the Department of Labor. The WHD is the agency of government responsible for protecting workers from violations of the law concerning compensation. Analyzing not only existing cases, but also posing as fictitious workers and employers, the GAO studied the performance of the WHD in responding to the most common forms of wage theft. The results were shocking—revealing an agency not only inadequately staffed but also mishandling cries for help, sometimes demonstrating gross negligence and even fraud. For example,

- Of the ten fictitious cases, only one was judged to be handled appropriately. Three of these cases were never investigated, including one that alleged children were operating dangerous heavy machinery during school hours.[10]
- In several real and fictitious cases, when employers agreed to pay back stolen wages, cases were closed without verifying that the wages were paid—even when complainants called

back several times to complain that they had not received the wages.[11] In one actual case, an employer offered to pay for minimum wage and overtime violations but not for stolen tips. WHD did not accept the offer but closed the case without pursuing the stolen tips.[12]

- If employers refuse to pay back stolen wages, WHD staff can recommend to their supervisors that the case receive a full, in-depth investigation. But in two out of the three fictitious cases in which an employer refused to pay, staff simply told complainants they had a right to sue if they wanted. One investigator responded to pleas for more help by responding, "I've done what I can do, I've asked her to pay you and she can't . . . I can't wring blood from a stone," and then suggested the complainant contact his representative in Congress to ask for increased funding for WHD.

- Some investigators lied to complainants about progress on their cases or the reasons for lack of progress.[13]

- In one actual case, two garment workers filed complaints "alleging that their former employer did not pay minimum wage and overtime to its workers."[14] In its investigation, WHD learned the employer made employees sign a document attesting that they had been paid "in compliance with the law" before receiving their paychecks. On the next day, an investigator went to the factory and took pictures. No further action was taken until two months later when a second investigator went to the factory. It was empty! A realty broker in the area said that he did not believe the company had relocated, so WHD declared the case closed. GAO auditors working on this report quickly found the factory, three miles away, using publicly available documents.[15]

If you haven't already guessed, WHD has a serious backlog of cases, which precludes initiating investigations within six months. GAO investigators found backlogs of seven to eight months at one regional WHD office and thirteen months in another.[16] These backlogs are troubling because the federal statute of limitations to collect back wages under the Fair Labor Standards Act is "two years from the date of the employer's failure to pay the correct wages."[17] However unfair this provision may sound, given the backlog of cases, federal courts still enforce the statute of limitations.

Because of the lack of law enforcement, an unfair choice is put before those employers who do comply with the law. They can continue to obey the law, but face competition from those who lower their operating costs through wage theft, or they can adopt the same methods in order to stay competitive. The lack of enforcement of existing law therefore tends to increase the incidence of wage theft and therefore the need for workers centers.

The number of workers centers in the United States grew exponentially in the 1990s and earliest years of the twenty-first century, as steady streams of migrants, authorized and not, arrived from Latin America. These new workers clustered in service sectors, poultry, meatpacking, and agriculture. Faith communities joined with social service providers in many areas to sponsor these "mediating institutions" to help workers learn their rights, organize for specific campaigns, and find legal help for violations of labor law. Workers centers affiliated with faith communities also benefit from allied clergy and laity who may assist workers seeking justice.

As the case against Spic and Span proceeded, other *Fe y Justicia* worker leaders and many former wage theft victims took aim at public policy. The laws on the books simply weren't enough—wage theft offenders needed to face real consequences. Julia DeLeon, a nanny, and Martin Mares, a construction worker, both former wage theft victims, collected petition signatures in apartment complexes and health fairs for a wage theft ordinance that would bar offenders from receiving forty-six types of city permits for five years. In reality, if a business lost all of its operating permits, it would be forced to close down. If the ordinance passed, the city of Houston would also prohibit the hiring of individuals or firms assessed penalties for wage theft offenses.

Julia and Martin organized worker visits to city councilors. They publicized the ordinance at both worker and community events and gave presentations at Rice and other local universities. They successfully engaged the local news media, empowering other wage theft victims to tell their stories to an increasingly concerned public. Negotiations with councilors and business leaders brought some concessions: only those business owners *criminally* convicted of wage theft (not simply losing in small claims court) would lose permits, and an employer would have to renege on paying a civil judgment to be placed on the city's "do-not-hire" list.

But the proposed ordinance's premise remained: wage theft would not be tolerated by the city of Houston. On November 19, 2013, Houston's wage theft ordinance passed unanimously. Today, *Fe y Justicia*'s leaders like Julia and Martin have no illusions about the ordinance—they do not believe it will put a total end to wage theft. They do, however, think its passage could provide them with another tool in their campaign to hold employers accountable to existing minimum wage and overtime laws. "It's not just having the victory," Martin said, "It's making sure it's implemented. We now need to ensure it gets enforced."

Wage theft remains a core concern in nearly every workers center in the country. But enforcing existing labor laws like the minimum wage is not enough. A minimum wage worker is a person living in poverty in most every scenario except a single person living alone. For example, a single parent living with one child earning minimum wage earns $15,080 per year working forty hours per week. That's still almost a thousand dollars below the poverty line. Add more children and the situation grows bleaker.

Each passing year dilutes the purchasing power of a minimum wage job, even with inflation moderately in check. To equal its purchasing power in 1968, today's $7.25 minimum wage would need to be raised to $10.69.[18] For minimum wage workers living in poverty or just above it, the choice is always which budget items to forgo each month. Will it be food? Paying the rent?

Purchasing medicine? School supplies for children? Minnesota's Twin Cities' workers center, Centro de Trabajadores Unidos en Lucha (The Center of Workers United in Struggle, or CTUL) took this question on after its wage theft efforts succeeded, but its members remained mired in poverty.

Justice for Janitors, Continued

Maricela Flores took a deep breath as she entered the hotel conference room. She had come a long way from Minnesota's Twin Cities to the Target Corporation's annual shareholders meeting in Denver. Today she would not be working the 4:00 a.m. shift polishing a Target store's floors or sprucing up its bathrooms. She would instead represent hundreds of fellow janitors, organized through CTUL at a meeting with high-level executives, including Target's general counsel, the culmination of CTUL's four-year Campaign for Justice in Retail Cleaning.

For Maricela, the meeting was an opportunity to tell her story on behalf of other workers. She and her husband emigrated from Mexico in 1993, gradually bringing over her parents, brothers, and sisters. Now single and raising four children on her own, living in a trailer with another family, Maricela cleans a Target store in Shakopee, Minnesota, for a company called Carlson Building Maintenance. Target and most large retail stores do not employ any janitors of their own—they subcontract the cleaning of every store. Some of these contractors, in turn, subcontract to other companies, and the retail stores take no responsibility for their actions. Herein lay the problem. Maricela knew of twenty workers cleaning K-Mart stores in the Twin Cities metro area, whose paychecks simply vanished, in 2009, when a subcontractor of Diversified Maintenance Systems (DMS), K-Mart's janitorial services contractor, itself disappeared. DMS refused to cover the wages, insisting they had no responsibility for the missing earnings. CTUL led a delegation of workers to K-Mart to share their stories of wage theft at the hands of their employer, and DMS reversed course within a couple of months.

Maricela liked Target; she just couldn't afford to buy much in the store with her $8.00/hour wages. Every day brought difficult choices—what to buy, what to do without. Eight dollars an hour was her starting wage. Now it purchased less than ever—and certainly not the nice things she saw for sale as she cleaned the aisles of the Shakopee Target. "I ask myself," she said. "If I buy this article of clothing, will I have enough money left to buy meat for my family? Or if I buy meat for the week, will I have enough money to buy shoes or pants for the kids? Or if I buy both of them, will I end up owing on the rent?" In contrast to workers like Maricela who clean Target stores, the unionized janitors who service Target's corporate headquarters building in Minneapolis make a starting wage of $14.27/hour. Veteran retail janitors shared with Maricela that fifteen years ago, wages were $10–11/hour, and there were twice as many workers cleaning each store.

Maricela's working conditions were also a challenge, as she frequently utilized dangerous industrial cleaning chemicals. By the end of a shift, she often felt nauseous. It often seemed as if she herself was regarded as a cleaning machine, a futuristic cyborg, always on call. Carlson demanded she work seven days per week, with no days off for illness or for a child's sickness. "They always say, 'That's the way it's going to stay,'" she added.

At CTUL, Maricela met other workers with similar experiences—poorly paid, exposed to noxious chemicals, and forced to work every day of the week. Some even received *less* than minimum wage! Conversations among the workers built solidarity and the courage for action: first on wage theft, then on working conditions for retail janitors. Ultimately, they would try to increase wages, building on smaller successes.

One of the workers Maricela met at CTUL was LeRoy Graham. LeRoy had moved from Arkansas to the Twin Cities in 1970, part of one of the great migrations of African Americans within the United States. He worked at an antenna factory for thirty years. When he retired, LeRoy soon found that his company pension was not enough to make ends meet, so he applied to work with DMS, cleaning a Target store in Columbia Heights, Minnesota, on the outskirts of Minneapolis. He hoped to use his earnings to finance some culinary training and open a catering business.

LeRoy enjoyed the sense of worker solidarity and empowerment he found at CTUL. He began to set up 1:1 meetings with fellow workers and invited them to become involved in the workers center. He felt his heart grow as he spoke to other workers and began to ponder a dramatic move. "I want to send my co-workers a love letter," he explained. "I want to send them a letter saying, 'In order to love, you have to love yourself.'"

LeRoy and Maricela took this message to fellow workers throughout 2012 and 2013. CTUL then led a series of three janitors' strikes against cleaning companies who service Target stores throughout the Twin Cities metropolitan area. Its activity culminated in a Black Friday (the day after Thanksgiving, traditionally the start of the Christmas shopping season), 2013, strike with a picket in front of Target's flagship store in downtown Minneapolis. A march followed, calling for fair wages in St. Paul. Over a thousand people turned out for the march. Sources within Target told CTUL that the workers' message was beginning to have an impact.

"The Black Friday strike was a lot of fun," recalled LeRoy. "We got training in what to expect and how to act. I've never done anything like this before." When LeRoy and twenty-five other workers and community allies sat in the street, police arrested them, but this was what the workers intended. They wanted to send a strong message—they were tired of wages that kept them in poverty, seven-day workweeks, wage theft, and no sick days, to the point they were willing to be arrested for civil disobedience.

Maricela received some pushback for her participation. A few friends and acquaintances asked, "How can you go out on strike when you've got four children to take care of?" She responded, "It is *because* of my children that I went on strike!" Twice during the campaign, Carlson fired Maricela, only to rehire her under pressure from CTUL and allied clergy.

During the second strike of the summer of 2013, CTUL secured the meeting in Denver with Target executives. Maricela recalled, "I was nervous before the meeting because I was afraid they would talk to us like our supervisors talk to us—mean and dismissive. When we got there, I actually got a chance to talk about all the problems my co-workers and I face cleaning their stores. It felt really good to be able to say these things out loud to people who I know could make a difference. They weren't mean to us. They listened to us."

Conversations between CTUL and Target continued until Target announced new terms that would become part of contracts with janitorial services. These provisions include the following:

- Vendors are not allowed to force employees to work seven days per week.
- Vendors are required to set up joint labor–management safety committees.
- Vendors must commit to eliminating wage theft.
- Vendors have six months after gaining a contract with Target to negotiate with and enter into an agreement with workers and a union, establishing a clear path for workers to gain union representation.

LeRoy, Maricela, and other workers associated with CTUL were ecstatic. The new safety committees would provide a venue to explore the many worker health issues connected to the use of hazardous chemicals, and potential unionization might lead to wages comparable to the unionized office janitors.

Maricela wrote a reflection on the campaign, widely read on the Internet, and excerpted in the print media:

When we started this, so many of us were afraid. I was afraid. This victory will give strength to anyone who has lived with this fear. I cry because I am happy that I can help people move away from fear and suspicion, to being organized and working towards victories collectively. We are human beings—when we get attacked, we rise together for good things. We have to do it for ourselves and for the future of our children.[19]

Maricela and LeRoy became active in CTUL out of love—love for children, love for other workers, and love of justice. Such motivations undergird the efforts of American workers centers, from the janitors of the Twin Cities to poultry workers in north-west Arkansas.

Arkansas Poultry Workers Find Their Voice

Marlem Diaz stared at the headless chicken hanging in front of her. She would not have much time to make the proper cuts. Several months previously, Simmons Foods sped up the line in their Springdale, Arkansas, poultry processing plant by 50 percent. When Marlem first arrived, nine years earlier, six people worked the line. Now, four did the work of six, deboning chicken for supermarket "pillow packs" of boneless breasts and thighs.

Marlem scanned the bird for rotten parts and quickly cut a few off. Then she grabbed the left wing, cutting it with a slice from the back. She pulled the right wing and did the same. The chicken proceeded down the line to her colleague, Shirley Lucky, an immigrant from the Marshall Islands, who completed the operation by cutting the wings off with a saw, leaving the chicken breast hanging for the next worker on the line.

When Marlem emigrated from Toluca, Mexico—a harrowing journey during which she and her daughters were kidnapped for three days—Arkansas poultry workers were mostly Hispanics, laboring alongside a handful of African Americans and older whites who were hanging on until retirement benefits kicked in. Only a few Marshallese worked the line. But as greater storm surges brought encroaching salt waters from the Pacific onto the Marshall Islands, and drought decimated its crops, local agricultural work began to disappear. Marshallese workers immigrated to northwest Arkansas in droves over the past decade, and now make up between 50 and 90 percent of the workforce in some poultry plants.

A sharp pain in Marlem's left hand brought a moment's distraction. The dull knife she wielded only made matters worse. With every incision she put more effort into cutting the wing loose, increasing the pressure on the joints in her hands. She performed this operation on forty-nine chickens per minute. Even with a sharp knife, the repetitive motion of the same chicken cuts, eight hours a day, for nine years, took its toll. Repeated trips to the company nurse offered no help. They applied massages, lotions, even hot wax treatments—none of these therapies mitigated the pain.

After nine years, Marlem gave up—her attempts to find a different kind of job at Simmons failed. In 2014, she resigned and took a job at competitor Southeast Poultry, a position requiring different cuts and motions, but she still found no relief. Her hands were permanently damaged.

"I talked to my husband," she said, "and he said, 'Look, they are demanding the work of four people out of three workers at Southeast—you're just going to ruin your hands even more. It's not going to do you any good.'" Marlem agonized over what to do. Poultry processing paid well. She made $12.00 per hour. Some workers, the fastest, made up to $15.00 per hour. But, she said, "I told my husband, it's with my hands that I am able to caress my kids." Marlem paused for a moment, choked back the tears and then continued: "I find it really hard to accept that I am asked to produce so much, while, at the same time, I am losing my abilities."

Marlem quit the new job within a month and is currently unemployed. With luck, she will pick up a retail job at minimum wage—$7.25 per hour. But her hands will likely never heal.

Hundreds of workers with such repetitive motion injuries eventually show up at the Northwest Arkansas Workers' Justice

Center (NWAWJC), asking for help. Women like Marlem show their swollen knuckles. Others, who remove chicken skin from the meat with their fingers, offer blackened areas under their fingernails, which commonly appear after about four years on the line. "In my former job," Marlem said, "I remember a co-worker who at one point developed a hole in her fingernail. The hole started penetrating through her entire finger, up to the point you could see a hole in it. She had it investigated by a doctor, and it was found to be cancer. She was laid off from the company. Eventually, she went back to her home in El Salvador to die."

One NWAWJC leader, Daniel Balanos, showed me his severed fingertips. While washing the empty but slowly moving line at 2:00 a.m. one morning in April 2013, Daniel grabbed a water hose to wash the work area. His hand caught on a spike intended for grabbing chicken necks and pulled his hand into other spikes designed to pull the chicken skin off. The line pulled Daniel's hand in. He described the incident: "I felt a big strong pinch in my fingers. At that moment, I just decided to pull my arm out as fast as I could. But at that time, it had already grabbed part of my fingers and chopped them off."

The machine was new; no signs alerted workers to potential dangers, though safety awareness signs (in English only) peppered the plant. Injected with painkillers, Daniel waited seven hours for surgery.

When he emerged from surgery, Daniel's supervisor was waiting for him. "Why did you stick your hand in there?" he asked. Daniel replied, "I didn't stick anything anywhere! I was washing the machine!" After a few weeks of continuing to receive his pay, Daniel was told not to come back to work unless he wished to return as a new employee at entry-level wages. Daniel is currently appealing his termination with the help of the NWAWJC.

Daniel introduced me to Gloria Diaz, originally from Guerrero, Mexico, who deboned chickens for Ozark Mountain Poultry so well, so quickly, that her supervisor frequently offered her fresh baked bread as a treat, on top of a $15.00/hour wage—until 2013, when she tore a disc in her back on the job. Her performance slowed, doctor visits multiplied, and the treats vanished. Gloria tried to manage the pain and continue working, but she developed fevers as well. When she became pregnant, the company doctor told her the symptoms were pregnancy related. She returned to a full load at work. One day, during her regular twelve-hour shift, Gloria reached for a chicken and "felt something in my back tear." She had ruptured a disc. She cried out in pain and was rushed to a local hospital.

The doctor attending to Gloria expressed concern about her pregnancy. He wrote a medical note stating that if Gloria did not address the ruptured disc and the pain it caused, she might compromise her pregnancy. "When I went to the human resources office," she said, "they told me, 'I'm sorry, Gloria. There's nothing I can do for you. I'm going to give you this phone number, a number within the company, that you can call and see if they can do anything for you, but I can't.'" No one responded to Gloria's phone message, and a week later, she lost her baby. Today, pumped up with painkillers and steroids, she continues to work the line, with little time to dwell on what might have been if she had carried her baby to term.

Marlem, Daniel, Gloria—each of their stories illustrates why poultry workers need a mediating institution to help them stand up to employers who view them as disposable commodities, workers who would receive gifts and praise when they performed faster than expected, but who would be laid off when their knuckles swelled so large they could not keep up with the line speed. Most poultry workers live in fear—fear they will be fired and blacklisted from working at *any* poultry plant if they speak up. Unauthorized Latino immigrants (by treaty, Marshallese are free to come to the United States as they please) also fear they will be deported and are therefore slow to voice their concerns.

Since 2002, the NWAWJC has provided a platform for poultry workers (and others—Wal-Mart workers are very active, as well) to tell their stories in local churches, to journalists, and to human rights organizations. The NWAWJC has also offered legal services, human rights education, and organizers to bring worker leaders together to act on their greatest concerns. Guiding all of these efforts is the principle that workers ought to control the decisions affecting their lives.

Workers active in the NWAWJC reported that its activities have helped them respond not only to their individual needs, but have also brought them fulfillment in working on the concerns of other workers, helping them find their voices. Gloria, for example, offered this reflection:

> When I first came, I was ignorant of my rights, I was ignorant about the things that were happening in my life. Then when I came and participated in the workshops, it just came to life. For example, that I would just clock in and put on my protective equipment, and that was three minutes that were not paid. I was learning how that time accumulates. It needs to be paid, but it wasn't being paid to me. Getting more involved helped strengthen my commitment to workers' rights.

Gloria became a leader at the NWAWJC out of her own need to stand up to wage theft and the sense that she herself had become a commodity in the poultry business. As her leadership skills grew, Gloria met workers with similar concerns, and she invited them into the NWAWJC.

Gloria, Marlem, and Daniel are each now active in the NWAWJC Justice for Poultry Workers Campaign. The NWAWJC has always helped workers with wage theft, Workers' Compensation, discrimination, and harassment cases. Now, after five years of organizing and $700,000 in back wages won, the NWAWJC has launched a campaign against the Obama Administration's Department of Agriculture's (USDA's) proposed new "Poultry Modernization" rules. These regulations would allow increased line speeds in poultry processing, raising the likelihood of worker injuries and inspectors missing more feces, bile, and scabs on chicken passing through the line. The poultry industry, for its part, promises to treat its chicken products with an additional antibacterial bleach solution to compensate. Although the health risks to consumers have been noted by the industry, poultry companies have said relatively little about worker safety.

In addition to getting the "Poultry Modernization" line speed changes dropped, NWAWJC leaders would like to see safety committees convened in each plant, to identify ways to prevent injuries and health problems. If such committees existed, Mercedes Rodriguez (pseudonym) might have found an exit sooner when an ammonia explosion rocked the Tyson Foods poultry plant in which she worked. "There was no exit sign," she explained, "and no trainings on how to evacuate the building whatsoever!" Since her ammonia exposure, Mercedes has been diagnosed with asthma, and she suffers from chronic nasal congestion as well as continuing acid reflux. Her Workers' Compensation case is proceeding, but her main interest is making sure other workers are not exposed to chemicals simply because they do not know the exit route.

NWAWJC Development and Communications Director Ana Aguayo views the Justice for Poultry Workers campaign as three pronged. First, workers see the line speed ruling as key, but it is a national, not just a local issue, so poultry workers and allies in other states must also speak out against the proposed USDA rules and encourage the Occupational Safety and Health Administration (OSHA) to bring its expertise to bear. Second, workers at Simmons Poultry (where Marlem worked) would like to negotiate an "ethical covenant" with the company, bringing greater attention to wage and health and safety issues in a formal way. This covenant could then stand as a model for other companies. Third, the campaign intends to educate and assist workers in developing health and safety committees to reflect on their current workplaces and determine how they can make them safer, much like the committees CTUL's leaders seek. Such committees, Ana explained, "ensure that those who are voiceless, those who are the most fearful in the community, have some pathway of support, when it comes to reporting health and safety issues." At one time, that pathway of support was provided by professional NWAWJC staff like Ana. Today, as the NWAWJC has matured, workers like Marlem, Daniel, and Gloria lead the way.

Gaining Respect, Weathering Attacks

Many community organizations like *Fe y Justicia*, CTUL, and NWAWJC begin life with an initial period of small victories before they attract the attention—or go after—a powerful opponent. The ensuing war of words, community meetings, and even lawsuits makes progress on issues of importance to vulnerable workers more difficult, but, at the same time, raises the stakes—and the possibilities of what can be accomplished. Many community organizers see attacks from powerful actors in public life as a badge of honor—it's a sign of an organization's effectiveness and its power, a token of respect.

Imagine then, the reaction of CTUL leaders like LeRoy and Maricela, when the U.S. Chamber of Commerce issued a blistering 2014 report, *The New Model of Representation: An Overview of Leading Workers Centers*, alleging that workers centers are clandestine fronts for unions and "engage in conduct—including protests, secondary boycotts, and other picketing activities—that would likely be unlawful under the National Labor Relations Act if done by traditional labor unions."[20] The report gives a nod to the "historical mission"[21] of workers centers (providing various services to workers and raising awareness of worker rights), but then asserts that workers centers today simply exist to grow the labor movement by funneling low-wage workers into union memberships, while posing as "grassroots movements."[22]

To substantiate its allegations against CTUL, the Chamber of Commerce report offered specious evidence, noting, for example, that CTUL organizer Brian Payne once worked for a union.[23] The document also pointed out that the president of the Service Employees International Union, Local 26, joined CTUL members partway into a May 2011 twelve-day hunger strike,

"Hungering for Justice."[24] His union also sent representatives to other CTUL actions against cleaning companies working for Target.[25] The report also alleges that no janitors were present at these actions in support of janitors, a point LeRoy, Maricela, and the police officers photographed arresting LeRoy (page 62) would dispute.[26]

A neutral observer might note that unions and workers centers both care about workers and sometimes collaborate based on mutual interests. Someone familiar with labor history might also point out that workers centers emerged because unions weren't doing a very good job at organizing low-wage workers, particularly in sectors dominated by unauthorized immigrant workforces. To conclude that just as workers centers begin to achieve a modicum of success, they would pivot to promoting union membership is to miss entirely why workers centers exist at all. When workers like Zenaida, LeRoy, and Marlem looked for help, unions were not there for them—but workers centers responded. Workers centers have become the mediating institution for "the excluded" worker, unprotected by the labor movement, and have achieved victories on their own terms that surpass the successes of many unions.

In over two hundred communities, workers centers have provided an important new voice for low-wage workers. The Chamber of Commerce report acknowledges they have developed some power. But workers centers are not the only vehicle for worker justice. In California, domestic workers have fought back against the injustices encountered by housecleaners like Zenaida with a tool that most certainly would receive the endorsement of the Chamber of Commerce: they formed their own company.

WAGES: Achieving Living Wages through Worker-Owned Enterprises

Maria Lucero was always the quiet one—a worker who did as she was told, without much fuss, in a series of low-wage jobs: babysitter, meat cutter, restaurant worker, and hotel cleaner.

That all changed when she developed allergies, sore throats, and burning eyes from the harsh chemicals she used on the job at the hotel. When her son developed some of the same symptoms in 2008, most likely from her contaminated clothing, she approached the Michael Chavez Center in Concord, California, a multiservice center operating in one of the poorest neighborhoods of the Bay Area.

"I was looking for a cleaning model that did not use these chemicals," she said. Coincidentally, staff at the Chavez Center had been looking for women with cleaning experience to launch a worker-owned "green" home cleaning cooperative embracing all-natural cleansers. Maria became a founding member of Contra Costa Natural Home Cleaning. Immediately, her wages almost doubled, from $7.25 per hour to $14.00 per hour. Working with three other women, she discovered what it means to be an *owner* as well as a worker.

"The difference is that everyone has an equal say," she explained. "There is no boss, no one on top, and that takes away a lot of our fear. We do have a manager, but there is no fear that this person will retaliate against us if there is something wrong with our work." Cleaning houses in Contra Costa County, Maria now works a living wage job, and the family's allergy symptoms have disappeared. In 2010, when Contra Costa Natural Home Cleaning joined the Women's Action to Gain Economic Security (WAGES) network of cooperatives, Maria expanded her circle of colleagues to nearly one hundred worker-owners of five cleaning cooperatives throughout California's Bay Area.

Through her participation in the WAGES network, with its varied professional development offerings, Maria has also grown as a leader, speaking out on the job about the business and developing new skills. She explained, "I didn't know how to drive, but first I had to overcome my fear. And I'm learning from all of the trainings WAGES offers—how to lead the business, deal with the different personalities, and work as a team. But the most important thing is that I'm not quiet anymore. I've gained a lot of confidence knowing that I'm being heard, what I say is being taken into account, and what I say can help solve problems."

Maria's experience of material and human development is not unique. In the WAGES cleaning cooperatives, on average, women increased their household income from $24,000 to nearly $41,000 annually, above average for Hispanic households nationwide. Worker owners also receive benefits like medical and dental insurance, short- and long-term disability insurance, and paid time off, many for the first time in their lives. In addition, WAGES has provided referrals for human services, Individual Development Accounts (IDAs—bank accounts for low-income people that provide matching funds for their deposits), and no-interest loans to promote human and material asset development.

Maria now wishes to share her experience with other women working low-wage jobs, struggling to exit the cycle of poverty. She dreams of her company expanding, building on the growing popularity of all-natural cleaning products. Her cooperative received renewed attention along with new customers when it won a 2012 Leader in Sustainability Award from the environmental organization Sustainable Contra Costa.

Within the WAGES network, a new worker-owned cooperative is also about to be launched—a business that will produce and sell *paletas*, multiflavored Latin American ice pops (be sure to try the "spicy cucumber and lime"!). Demonstrating success with other worker-owned businesses will expand WAGES' effectiveness, indicating the viability of worker-owned cooperatives in other sectors of the economy and showing that sometimes workers can fight back against poverty wages, minimal benefits, and wage theft by launching their own business.

Beyond Empowerment

When anthropologist Steve Striffler reflected on his 2003 experience "undercover" in an Arkansas poultry plant,[27] he shared a poignant—and funny—story of worker solidarity. On a lunch break, a group of Mexican co-workers declared him a Mexican (not just an honorary Mexican), because he worked hard and ate lunch with Mexicans. "It's pure Mexicans here," one colleague said. A Salvadoran woman protested, but then she came to understand the term as meaning "exploited worker," which, to her, felt accurate. The group then decided to include a Laotian woman who did not always mix with them. Despite her reserve, she, too, was deemed a Mexican.

Their dialogue was comical, but the point was clear—worker solidarity can dissolve racial/ethnic tensions. Journalists covering immigration may chatter on about discord between black and brown in the workplace, but LeRoy and Maricela at CTUL moved in a different direction, focusing on their common interests and developing a friendship that crossed the racial divide. Back in northwest Arkansas, poultry companies are beginning to alternate Latinos and Marshallese on the processing line, a "divide and conquer" tactic aimed at limiting conversations among colleagues. The NWAWJC is alert to this strategy, promoting dialogues between Latino and Marshallese workers to bridge the cultural differences between these two key populations of poultry workers.

The impact of worker solidarity on racial/ethnic divisions among workers calls to mind Galatians 3:28: "There is no longer Jew or Greek, there is no longer slave or free, there is no longer male and female; for all of you are one in Christ Jesus." When these centers organize workers in struggles for justice, they empower them to speak out, to learn the tools of public action, and utilize them effectively in the public arena. But it doesn't stop there. At the level of worker solidarity, racial and ethnic differences among workers become permeable, and true friendship, even fraternity, develops. This is perhaps the greatest potential of workers centers, beyond empowerment. As our pilgrimage spiritual director Pope Francis noted, in his 2014 World Day of Peace message, "without fraternity, it is impossible to build a just society and a solid and lasting peace."[28]

This message has not been lost on the community of people with disabilities. Far north of Arkansas, in the suburbs of Chicago,

Progress Center for Independent Living—one of many Centers for Independent Living across the United States—people with varied disabilities come together as one community to promote fraternity and the same rights of access that people without disabilities enjoy. Our pilgrimage shifts to the north as we join the diverse yet united group of advocates at Progress Center.

Chapter 4

"Who's Got the Tickets?": Progress Center for Independent Living

The poor not only suffer injustice but they also struggle against it! They are not content with empty promises, excuses or alibis. Neither are they waiting with folded arms for the aid of NGOs, welfare plans or solutions that never come or, if they do come, they arrive in such a way that they go in one direction, either to anaesthetize or to domesticate. This is a dangerous means. You feel that the poor will no longer wait; they want to be protagonists; they organize themselves, study, work, claim and, above all, practice that very special solidarity that exists among those who suffer, among the poor, whom our civilization seems to have forgotten, or at least really like to forget.

—Pope Francis
Address to World Meeting of
Popular Movements, October 25, 2014

Henry Boyce's smooth baritone charmed women and men alike in the Chicago nightclub scene of the early 1970s. Men wanted to be his friend; women wanted to date him. "Up and down State Street, everyone knew me," he said. Henry and his

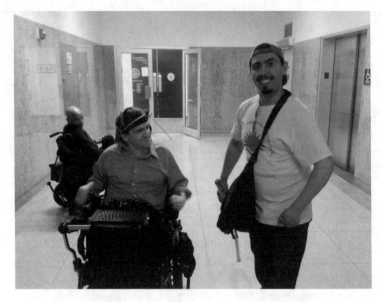

*Activist Larry Biondi runs into a former Progress Center
intern lobbying for charter schools at the Illinois Capitol building.*

band played mostly covers, soul music with occasional forays
into pop, particularly Beatles songs. The Spirit of '76 nightclub
provided a regular venue, and a growing fan base cried, "You
gotta make a record!"

But as the '70s wore on, Henry's body wore out. Alcohol,
marijuana, and cocaine became a central part of his life. His
musical creativity and leadership skills faded. The 1980s brought
a downhill slide into a life of addiction, poverty, and homelessness. Then the falls began.

"I thought it was equilibrium problems at first," he explained,
"but I began to fall down more and more frequently. My hands
started shaking and my voice started to get different, raspy and
hard to understand." I leaned in, listening closely. Henry *is* difficult to understand. His voice sounds a bit like someone who
has undergone a tracheotomy and speaks through a hole in his or
her neck. But after ten minutes, I found I understand every word.

Before long, Henry lost the ability to walk. Depressed and confined to a wheelchair, he refused to take a bath or shower for three years. "At first, I didn't know how to handle this," he said. "I was like, 'I'm through—I'm finished.' I was a singer, and that hurt too. Singing was a gift—and I couldn't use it no more. So my fall was much harder than if I didn't have that talent. When that gift wasn't there, I wasn't *me*."

Lying in bed or sitting in his wheelchair most days, Henry thought of his family and friends. But warm thoughts did not follow. Only rage.

"At first I was sad and pitiful, but then I got *angry!*" he said. "Angry at how people could lie to me and tell me they're going to take me to a doctor's appointment and then don't show up until three or four hours late, and then expect me to be happy! That's what really broke my heart. When people said they would help me, and they never did. You can't depend on other people; they've got their lives, too, you know."

Where was his entourage? What happened to the people who used to greet him walking down State Street? His family? Gone, just gone.

"I realized that it was on me," he explained. "I had to decide if I wanted to be a man or something less. So I looked in the mirror one day and said, 'You are more than this. You are more than someone who just don't matter.'"

Henry began his comeback around 2008. He quit drinking. He began to practice smiling. Previously a snappy dresser, he found bargains on suits, hats, and shoes that still looked like a million bucks. He enrolled in Chicago's Malcom X College, majoring in addiction studies, wearing a suit and tie every day. After all he'd been through, Henry thought he'd make a good addictions counselor.

Entering a classroom for the first time in decades, Henry immediately felt forty pairs of eyes boring into him: "When I went to class, I know it was on everyone's mind—who is this guy? I was sixty-three years old at the time, sixty-seven now. We had a project, and the professor told us to split into groups of six.

So I noticed nobody wanted to get with me. And the professor said, 'Look, somebody's got to get into a group with Mr. Boyce.' And that made me feel like 'Hey, wait a minute!' Then, after we finished the project and everyone's grades came around, the next project we did, everyone wanted to get with my group! That was beautiful!" he said, laughing.

Upon graduation, Henry started looking for a job or internship to begin his career as an addictions counselor, and the awkward discrimination started all over again. His 3.6 grade point average would get him a callback, but his voice—the voice that had once enthralled audiences all over Chicago—frightened off potential employers.

Discouraged, Henry turned to Progress Center for Independent Living, one of over four hundred loosely affiliated community-based service and advocacy centers operated by and for people with disabilities across the United States. Progress Center serves 113 municipalities in suburban Cook County, near Chicago. It strives to promote civil rights for people with disabilities, de-institutionalization, de-medicalization, and the removal of barriers to self-sufficiency.

A receptionist, accustomed to directing consumers to specific services (the Progress Centers do not serve clients; they serve *consumers*, who decide what is best for themselves), approached executive director Horacio Esparza after meeting Henry. "He needs some advice," she said. "He wants to know if somebody can help him, and I don't know who can help him. To whom should I refer him?"

"Let me talk to Mr. Boyce," responded Horacio. Henry wheeled in and shared his story, adding his frustrations at not finding a job or internship. "Henry, what took you so long to come here?" Horacio asked, a dash of playful agitation in his voice. Then he addressed Henry's concerns. "First, they should not turn you down. You need to talk about your accommodations." Sizing Henry up, he added, "They don't know what they are missing. Your time is very valuable for us. You can do an internship with us, and we're going to pay you for that internship. Send a letter to the organization that is turning you down. But, *you* are going to turn *them* down, because you've got something better."

Elated, Henry wheeled over to advocacy coordinator Larry Biondi's office. Larry explained to Henry the components of the legislative training, "How to Be a Self Advocate," that kicked off the internship. Over a two-month period, Henry would learn how a bill becomes a law, how to lobby, key times to lobby, how to make his vote count, and how to tell politicians what services should be in the budget for people with disabilities. The training would include a "lab" experience, a trip to the Illinois State Capitol in Springfield.

Larry also showed Henry the speech machine he uses to offset the effects of cerebral palsy on his ability to communicate. He gave Henry the contact information for University of Chicago technicians who could equip Henry with a similar machine. At the start of our interview, Henry demonstrated how the speech machine worked, a tablet computer connected to a speaker installed on his wheelchair. Henry typed in what he wanted to say, and a preselected computer voice read the text. Henry answered my first question using the machine.

I stopped the interview. I didn't think the voice sounded like Henry. I couldn't tell you why; it just wasn't right. Then I blurted out a rude question: "Henry, why did you choose to sound like a white guy from California?" He considered my question, for a moment. Then he burst out laughing, and disconnected the machine.

At first I wondered if the manufacturer only gave him one choice, but Henry explained that he had strategically chosen that particular voice. Informed by his long experience working with crowds and sitting at the intersection of race and disability discrimination, Henry was shrewdly connecting to his audience. "For most of the audiences I speak to," he said, "that's the language they're used to hearing. They hear this and relax and say, 'This sounds like something we can relate to.'"

Henry excelled in his internship, relating well with legislators, holding them accountable, and inspiring other consumers to speak out in public life. Drawing on his experiences from the internship and as a self-described "advocate" during the Civil rights movement, Henry put much of his passion into the issue of housing. He is fortunate in that regard, living in a subsidized, accessible apartment in Oak Park, but it was hard work getting that apartment, and now he hopes to help other consumers.

"You've got to organize," he explained. "We're more or less not included in the housing market—and we need to be! And I have heard some of the sad stories people with disabilities have told about nursing homes. You've got someone taking all but a certain percentage of your income. You've got to be in at a certain time. A lot of time, people are being abused. It's like in the Bible, the King of Egypt, Pharaoh. Way back when he had the Jews, and he wouldn't let them go. He said, 'Hey, this is profitable!' With nursing homes, all you have to do is provide the minimum—put a roof over my head, give me a bed to sleep in. The regulations don't say what the condition of the place has to be. And it doesn't matter if you're intelligent or not—you're treated like you're not! I have to be concerned about it. I've never lived in a nursing home, but I've been inside them—the lack of independence, the monitoring."

Recently appointed to Progress Center's board of directors, Henry has quickly learned the fullness of "disability culture," a term that refers to the group identity emerging from so many people with disabilities sharing experiences of oppression and resilience. Disability culture encompasses a strong pride in personhood, as one's disability becomes an integral part of that person's identity.

Henry approaches his advocacy work first with an attempt to establish rapport—with legislators, legislative staff, and consumers. He has found public officials generally responsive to that style. "But what we need is for them to respond to what we see the issues are and what we need, and to understand that we vote. The vote is our power," he said. "We are not asking for anything that everybody else is not getting. We are just asking for what everybody else is getting. We want to be able to go into a restaurant and sit down at the table with everybody else, and not have a table in the closet where people with disabilities eat." Henry's commentary evokes, once again, the words of Pope Francis, calling Catholics to reach out in fraternity to the excluded.

The Challenge:
Stigmatization, Discrimination, and Poverty

"If you don't defend your civil rights, they go away," stated Progress Center information and referral/benefit specialist Anne Gunter, drawing together the disparate challenges faced by people with disabilities. The struggles of consumers like Henry are especially poignant: they ask society to change only insofar as to allow them to enjoy the same kind of lives fully abled people already have, a demand Henry might have made in his days with the civil rights movement. They want to be hired if they are the most qualified for a job. They want to be treated like a valued customer when they go into a store. They want to live in the community and not in an institution, in a home they can enter and move about with ease. They want respect.

Saint John Paul II once observed, "human work is *a key*, probably *the essential key*, to the whole social question."[1] By extension, work is also the key to Integral Human Development. Work helps people feel worthwhile; it is a creative outlet. Work provides remuneration to attend to a host of personal needs and to invest in one's continued development. John Paul didn't stop there, noting that through work, humans participate in God's ongoing creation of the universe.[2] Helping disabled people find meaningful work is therefore an essential part of Progress Center's mission, an element that brings staff like Horacio face-to-face with employment discrimination.

"About three months ago," he explained, "a young bilingual lady named Maribel came to me and told me about her latest

#1 HR essue "Future of Work
+ Fair Pay - Less inequity

job search. She said, 'I got up at five o'clock in the morning. I completed everything by Internet and it sounded like I was hired.' As soon as she got to the interview, when they saw she was in a wheelchair, they told her, 'Oh, sorry, we just filled the position.' How can you have filled a position when that very same morning you sent an e-mail saying, 'We are waiting for you'?"

Maribel checked on the company's website a few days later and found the position still advertised. Horacio connected her with an organization called Equipped for Equality that specializes in legal assistance for people with disabilities. A lawsuit is now making its way through the legal system, but Maribel does not want a settlement—she wants a job.

Most Progress Center leaders whom I interviewed told similar stories—even Bruce Paul, a current legislative advocacy intern with a Ph.D. in physics. Saint John Paul II's insight seems all the more prescient in the context of widespread poverty among people with disabilities. Horacio spends a great deal of time puzzling over this essential problem of employment. He therefore has a hard time listening to the typical media profiles of people with disabilities. "They'll describe them like heroes," he said. "'Oh, they are so *smart!*' or 'He's blind, *but he's very smart!*' or they'll tell you, 'Oh, you're *smarter* than me.' But if you ask them for a job, then they won't believe you are smart. They show these stories on TV, and I don't like them! I don't want to hear those stories. I want to hear a story from an *employer* saying, 'I gave a job to this person.' Then, they will be showing that they believe we are capable."

Even Horacio, who now holds a high-level nonprofit management position, came up short in his attempts to secure employment outside of disability organizations. As a young man, he earned a bachelor's degree in Hispanic literature at a university in Mexico. He wrote a book of poetry in 1986 and worked in Mexico for the Department of Education and Culture, playing keyboard in a band on nights and weekends.

Living in the United States in the early 1990s, Horacio was unable to find work in the arts, so he and his family lived off of

Social Security disability payments. He formed a support group, Latinos Vision Impaired of Illinois. On a volunteer basis, he taught Braille, mobility orientation, and daily living skills to visually impaired Latinos. In 1999, his son's retina detached, causing blindness, just as his own retina had when he was a young man. Horacio felt an even stronger calling: he would make advocacy for people with disabilities his life's project.

When Horacio's youngest daughter experienced a retinal detachment four years later, it only confirmed his vocation. First hired as the independent living coordinator for Progress Center's satellite office in the predominantly Latino town of Blue Island, then as its regional director, Horacio was invited to become the organization's executive director in 2008, overseeing programs of both systemic change like legislative advocacy and direct services such as teaching independent living skills, providing information and referral, and facilitating peer counseling.

In many ways, Progress Center embodies the Catholic social teaching principles expressed in the popular catechetical tool "The Two Feet of Love in Action." One foot represents "social justice (addressing systemic, root causes of problems that affect many people),"[3] and the other stands for "charitable works (short-term, emergency assistance for individuals)."[4] Both "feet" are needed to move toward the Kingdom of God, and their relationship is complementary.

At Progress Center, a consumer will often come in for the life skills class "Let's Live," learning what they need to know about independent living, from budgeting to job hunting to traveling. Then they might graduate to the legislative advocacy training program. For a few, like Clark Craig, now working with Larry as community organizing advocate, the internship leads to employment at Progress Center itself. Progress Center's direct services therefore address the needs of the consumers who come seeking help, but they also surface *leaders*, like Henry and Clark, who develop into Board members and staff.

Consumers come to Progress Center with a variety of disabilities.

Some have mobility disorders, others hearing or sight impairments, still others cognitive disorders and mental illnesses. The staff, too, reflects this range of disabilities. They respond daily with their "two-feet," or "two-wheels."

In some cases, Progress Center simply helps consumers learn how to give appropriate social cues to the people around them, like Ernesto Mendez, who emigrated from Oaxaca, Mexico, in 1976, when he was twelve years old. When he was five years old, someone threw paint in Ernesto's eyes, burning a cornea. Blind in one eye, he tried to get by with partial vision, even faking it in the workplace, driving a forklift. Eventually confronted by company management, he reluctantly stepped down from his position and began collecting permanent disability insurance and Social Security. As his sight declined, Ernesto increasingly collided with people at random. Often, they responded angrily. "Sometimes they would want to fight with me because I hit them by accident or something," he recalled. "They would say, 'What's wrong with you?' I would say, 'Oh excuse me, I've got vision problems.' They would look at me like they didn't believe me."

Depressed and homebound, in 2011, Ernesto tuned into Horacio's weekly Spanish radio show, *Radio Vida Independente*. "When I heard Horacio on the radio, he sounded happy," he said. "He sounded like a normal person. He didn't care about the blindness!" Desperate, Ernesto called Horacio, who referred him to a conveniently located independent living class, where Ernesto learned how to use a cane in public.

Socially, the cane transformed Ernesto's life. "Now, if I'm going onto the bus, they always let me sit, because of my disability, when they see the cane," he said. "When I'm walking in the shopping mall, they never go against me. They always pull over to the side. When they teach you how to use a cane and how to walk through the people, everything changes—people respect you."

Growing in confidence, Ernesto began to take long walks, simply for the fitness benefits. Fluent in Braille, he studied to become a Braille instructor for undocumented immigrants ineligible for government services. He distributed canes obtained by Progress Center to sight-impaired Latinos living in the shadows, "excluded" from the social safety net. In a sense Ernesto became a volunteer emissary for Progress Center, helping disabled Latinos move toward independence.

Employment still remains elusive for Ernesto and close to 70 percent of working-age disabled people. For most disabled workers, long-term—even lifelong—unemployment means trying to survive on $600–700 per month from Social Security payments, plus whatever benefits from various local, state, and federal social welfare programs can be cobbled together. But even with these benefits, being disabled still means a life of poverty plus extra expenses because of one's disability.

The 2010 Census revealed that adults with disabilities aged twenty-one to sixty-four had average monthly earnings of $1,961, compared to $2,724 for those without disabilities. According to this most recent census, two million people are blind or unable to see, 1.1 million have severe hearing problems, seven million report severe depression or anxiety, 2.4 million have some form of dementia, 30.6 million reported difficulty walking or climbing stairs or used a wheelchair or cane, and 9.4 million noninstitutionalized adults reported difficulty with at least one activity of daily living (e.g., bathing, dressing, eating).[5]

As a group, people with disabilities now comprise over fifty-four million people, almost 20 percent of the population. "We are the biggest minority group in the country," boasts Horacio. "When elections come around, politicians will talk about listening to African Americans or Hispanics, but they never think about people with disabilities as a minority. We want them to start thinking of *us* as a *voting group*—fifty-four million people, plus our relatives and friends." Such thinking helped pass the Americans with Disabilities Act of 1990, which now prohibits discrimination based on disability in the workplace and public accommodations. Today, Progress Center seeks to increase disabled consumers' ability to act, to bring their power to the table of public life.

A Sleeping Giant Awakes

Loree Woodley grew up trailing her mother from one Urban League meeting to another. Quiet and introverted, she listened as Mrs. Woodley debated the hot issues of the '60s, '70s, and '80s with women and men concerned about the social problems African Americans experienced following the great migrations from the south to northern U.S. cities. That ability to listen has served her well as an advocate for people with disabilities and as president of the board of directors of Progress Center.

Loree's family came to Chicago in 1959 to pursue dreams of a vast real estate empire. Inspired by Chicago entrepreneur Dempsey Travis, who made a small fortune selling properties and arranging mortgages for African Americans seeking to buy homes in the Chicagoland area of the city from 1949 into the 1970s, Loree's father sought to achieve both economic and political power through property ownership. Immediately upon moving to Chicago, Mr. Woodley acquired four homes by stretching the family finances to the limit, and then died a year into the venture.

Devastated and lonely, Mrs. Woodley did not pack up and return to Oklahoma. She immersed herself in the Urban League, fighting Chicago's notorious redlining, moving into a white neighborhood, and earning income from the rental properties. Loree accompanied her mother to each meeting, a contrast to her extroverted mother—quiet, reserved, but always watching, listening, taking everything in.

At age fourteen, an ophthalmologist diagnosed Loree with *retinitis pigmentosa*, a genetic optical disorder that no one saw coming (Loree is adopted). She was not aware of symptoms at that point, but by her mid-twenties, she was having difficulty with night vision. Then, a decade later, her peripheral sight began to narrow. "Okay," she thought. "You're not seeing things peripherally. It's getting very dangerous here"—dangerous for Loree, but also for her preschool students. "They were beginning to run in and out of my field of vision," she recalled. "So after a couple of months, I talked to the parents about my situation."

Loree phased out of teaching in 1996 and began taking care of her aging mother, just as her own sight impairment worsened. Depression began to take hold even as caregiving demands increased. Her mother died in 2005, and shortly thereafter, Loree lost most of the rest of her functional vision, leaving her with just a small amount of light perception. Broke and homeless, she took to "camping out" in a friend's spare room. This experience of the dearth of affordable housing for the disabled made a strong impression—and she was from a family that once owned several properties!

During the same period, an acquaintance invited Loree to a meeting at Progress Center regarding transportation for disabled consumers. There she met organizer Sam Knight, who invited her to an open house, then a membership and outreach meeting. "I was coming to the meetings for about two years," she continued. Progress Center was just connecting to United Power for Action and Justice to get the Grove Apartments in Oak Park built with some units set aside for people with disabilities. I had a 1:1 with Amy, the organizer for United Power, and I was just kind of sharing my story. That activated the sleeping giant. The giant inside of me was asleep, until I had an opportunity to activate it by becoming involved in the challenge of housing for people with disabilities."

Lacking the power to accomplish all of its public policy goals on its own, Progress Center teamed up with the forty faith-based and community organizations that comprised United Power, an affiliate of the Industrial Areas Foundation (IAF) community organizing network. Together, they could engage in the battles each would not, singly, have a chance of winning—like getting accessible, affordable apartments for people with disabilities. Why was this effort so difficult? Meet the NIMBYs.

NIMBY means "Not in My Back Yard." The term emerged in the 1970s within the hazardous waste industry to describe residents who opposed local toxic waste disposal projects. NIMBY has since become much more broadly used to describe groups of typically middle-class neighbors who band together to oppose any number of developments, such as affordable housing for people living in poverty, housing for people with disabilities, infrastructure development like airports, commuter rail lines, power plants, electrical transmission lines, halfway houses for ex-convicts or addicts, solar or wind farms, crematoriums, even security lighting.

Reasons for opposition typically include fears of reduced property values, greater risk to community members, increases in crime, loss of a small town atmosphere, and disproportionate benefit to "outsiders." NIMBYs often make fair points, but if every community took their approach, we would have no places to process waste, and nowhere for people with various challenges and disabilities to live. Frequently, these developments end up being placed where poor and unorganized people live, itself an injustice.

Loree, representing Progress Center within United Power, took on the NIMBYs with the strongest weapon she had—her own story. She publicly shared her struggle with ever-encroaching blindness, her challenges with the Chicago Housing Authority and its constantly shifting eligibility rules for Senior Disability Buildings, and her experience with homelessness. She attended meetings with the Oak Park Housing Authority and Interfaith Housing Development Corporation to negotiate how the former Comcast building would be redeveloped. How many apartments would be accessible to people with disabilities? How many would be set aside for *any* low-income person or family?

Ultimately, these questions were resolved through two years of negotiations between United Power and the two parties. The building would be rehabilitated with ten units of affordable housing, meaning $690/month rent for a one bedroom apartment before subsidies. Twelve units would be specially designed with disability access in mind.

As the proposal shaped up, Loree prepared to fight the NIMBYs at a 2012 public meeting with the city's trustees at Oak Park's Ascension Church, first by listening. "So we heard what they had to say," she said. "Being involved in that helped me really begin to see that the problem with housing for people with disabilities is bigger than just us. It could be people who are in drug rehab programs or who are low-income but they're working." Loree added her testimony, emphasizing the common good in response. The Oak Park trustees voted to allow the project to move forward. Today, fifty-one families and individuals live in the Grove Apartments, and it is referred to as "once controversial" in the *Oak Park Sun Times*.[6] Loree was recently featured on an Archdiocese of Chicago video on the Catholic Campaign for Human Development, speaking about her development as a leader.

In the video, Loree mentioned becoming "empowered." She now credits former Progress Center organizer Sam Knight with persistently waking the sleeping giant. "Come on, Loree Woodley!" he implored. A significant victory for people with disabilities behind her, Loree believes she is now capable of actions she once thought impossible.

"The greatest thing I see for myself is not to be as hesitant," she said. "I'm more willing to push myself to be involved. There is still a sense of timidity there, but Progress Center has helped me to push it off. Now, I'll always be an advocate. I couldn't have said that two years ago."

Thinking about the future of her advocacy on disability issues, Loree believes she is called to work with young disabled advocates. She spent much of her youth observing Urban League leaders. Today, she listens carefully to all parties at a meeting and reflects for a time before offering her own opinion. Over time, Loree has developed what she calls an "intuitive gift, to look into a person, see their gifts, and then encourage them past any hesitancy, to let those gifts come right out."

With all humility, Loree shared her belief that one of the purposes of her life is, despite her blindness, to help people to see: "I can come into a group and sit and listen, and based on what I'm hearing, go through it and then say 'Here, I've seen this. This is also what I hear, from what you are saying,' or 'Maybe we can try doing it this way,' or, 'So you say you want to reach people, but maybe it's just not here.'" Physically, Loree can only see light and shadows, but she "sees" nuances in situations and overlooked options as well as the hidden capacities of other leaders. With quiet dignity, perseverance, and remarkable insight, she has found her own place in leadership, where a blind introvert can change the course of a meeting with one remark.

A Dreamer Comes of Age

Because no two persons are alike, no two persons' experiences of disability are the same. Each unique challenge is experienced through the prism of a one-of-a kind-soul in a singular place and time. Contrast Loree's story, then, to that of Gerardo Salinas, a "Dreamer" brought to the United States without authorization by his mother in 2001. The term "Dreamer" refers to immigrants who entered the country illegally before their sixteenth birthdays, but are not yet thirty-one years of age, are in school or graduated, or served in the military. They are generally seen as not responsible for the decision to come to the United States.

At the age of fourteen, Gerardo sat close to his mother and sister at the auditorium of Chicago's Rudy Lozano Library and listened intently to a 2001 presentation on blindness, hoping his family's recent illegal foray into the United States from Michoacán, Mexico, was not in vain. Surely the cure for his blindness would be found here, in one of America's great cities. His mother had heard as much—U.S. doctors, the best in the world, had found a cure for retinal detachment. As the speaker continued, Gerardo could sense his mother's growing anger.

Finally, Mrs. Salinas interrupted the speaker, Horacio Esparza, independent living coordinator at the time for Progress Center for Independent Living. "You know what?" she blurted out. "I didn't come for this! I came looking for medical treatment and a cure for my son!" Horacio asked why her son was blind and what treatments had been tried. Then he responded, "You know what? Your son is not going to be able to see. That's a reality. Retinal detachment is not reversible. I have been here for thirty years, and I have the same condition, retinal detachment. If there were a treatment, I would not be blind at this point."

Unwilling to give up on her dream of a cure, Mrs. Salinas collected her family and slipped out, but not before Horacio handed his business card to Gerardo. Mrs. Salinas threw it in the trash. Over the next four years, Gerardo muddled through a maze of services in the Chicago Public School system with no advocate, no mentor. He learned English and Braille, but otherwise felt on his own. Finally, he tracked Horacio down, to Progress Center's satellite office in Blue Island. Coincidentally, an open house was in session.

Staff and leaders introduced Gerardo to the many services offered to blind consumers. He became a Progress Center member and started coming to meetings, interacting with people with other disabilities. He began referring other undocumented Latinos to both Progress Center offices. In 2006, he was invited to begin the legislative internship.

Just as the open houses and independent living meetings opened up new possibilities in the area of services, the internship expanded Gerardo's view of what could be accomplished in the public square. "Before I had my internship, I thought it was very hard to make contact with legislators," he said. "I thought that, in order to make contact with them, you had to be like very powerful. Like a celebrity, somebody with power, being very important in the community. I said, 'No, they would never answer my phone calls or e-mails. No way.'"

"But, you know, I can call them or send them e-mails, and meet with them, and bring my topic, my issue, my concern, and work with them. Progress Center showed me that it was possible. I was able to meet with a couple of legislators. I still have great communication with them and meet with them about disability issues." Five years later, with Gerardo a legislative advocacy veteran, Progress Center put his skills to the test.

In 2011, the Illinois Home Services program was under attack. Half of the funds required to pay for personal assistants

(PAs) utilized by consumers with disabilities were cut in the draft state budget. PAs help people with disabilities with the basic activities of daily living: cooking, cleaning, getting to medical appointments, etc. During my weeklong visit to Progress Center, I watched as one PA assisted legislative advocacy coordinator Larry Biondi, who lacks full use of his arms and hands, in eating lunch. Without a PA, where would he go for help—a nursing home? And wouldn't those services cost more than a PA?

Gerardo trained Progress Center members to prepare them for the trip to the Capitol. They traveled by train to Springfield to bring their case for rescinding the cuts to the legislature. Three hundred people with disabilities crowded the lobby outside of the hearing room. The turnout, as well as the avalanche of e-mails, letters, and phone calls, caught the senators and representatives by surprise. They reversed course and restored the funds.

Legislative advocacy for people with disabilities is one of Gerardo's passions, but it isn't the only public issue he cares about. As a Dreamer, he is active with other organizations working on comprehensive immigration reform. Like most Dreamers, after having grown up in the United States, Gerardo is culturally American and wants to contribute to the nation both economically and socially. In 2007, Gerardo went to Washington, DC, to advocate for legislation to help Dreamers become citizens. Although the Dream Act failed to muster enough votes in Congress, the experience was exhilarating for Gerardo, and he continues to work on this and other immigration justice issues. In June 2012, the U.S. Secretary for Homeland Security announced a two-year, renewable reprieve from deportation for Dreamers like Gerardo. He got a Social Security number, a work permit, and a long-term chance at citizenship.

Gerardo sees a clear connection between disability issues and immigration justice. "Both are related," he said. "Because there are so many Dreamers and undocumented people with disabilities, you know. We cannot get all of the services that the Centers for Independent Living like Progress Center offer. We're still work-

ing on that with politicians, meeting and showing them stories
of disabled people who struggle because they are not citizens or
resident aliens and cannot get services."

Gerardo continued, identifying the personal cost of this inter-
section of exclusions. "There's adaptive technology that Progress
Center has, like computer screen readers," he said. "But in my case,
I'm not a resident alien or a citizen. I don't have access to that.
Agencies have the programs, the services, but we're not eligible."
Later, I mention Gerardo's point to Horacio. He is horrified.

"I just interviewed the assistant director of the Division of
Rehabilitative Services on my radio show," he said. "And I asked
him, 'What's happened? What are you doing for disabled Dreamers
who have work permits, but they don't have access to vocational
services?' He said, 'No, any citizen or resident of the United States,
or anyone who has a permit to work here, they should be able
to receive services.'"

Gerardo, standing ten feet away from us, but overhearing the
conversation, broke in. "I wasn't eligible. I asked them, and they
said 'No, because the law allows for you to get a job, but not the
services.'" Horacio repeated what he learned: "Well, I talked to
Francisco two weeks ago, and he said that if you have a permit
to be in the United States legally, you should be able to receive
services."

Immigration issues aside, the exchange I witnessed illustrated
a common problem. Sometimes disabled people do not know
the programs in which they may rightfully participate—even
someone as savvy and experienced as Gerardo. But even worse,
at times, *the people administering the programs* do not fully understand who is eligible. Consider the program administrator who
told Gerardo he was not eligible to utilize technology that would
help him become more employable. Was he deliberately cheating
Dreamers? More likely, he thought he was just doing his job in a
law-abiding way. The incident illustrated the need for organizations like Progress Center that mediate between individuals and
powerful forces in their lives, to both educate consumers with

disabilities about their rights *and* intervene when these rights are willfully or unwittingly ignored.

It was engaging the nuance of law, as well as the thrill of legislative advocacy, that inspired Gerardo to consider becoming a lawyer. Having completed his associate degree at City Colleges of Chicago in 2013, he entered the University of Illinois at Chicago as a political science major. From there, he plans to go to law school to become an immigration lawyer, with perhaps a stop in the field of social work on the way. Meanwhile, Gerardo will continue volunteering as a legislative advocacy trainer and motivational speaker for people with disabilities. From time to time he will speak at the Rudy Lozano Library and remember his own introduction to the Progress Center, noticing a young disabled teen sitting in his former seat.

A lawyer who is blind fighting for justice? It's hard not to think of Marvel Comics' superhero Daredevil, "The Man without Fear," whose alter ego, Matt Murdoch, lost his sight and gained his powers through a splash of radioactive waste. Hearing Gerardo's stories of climbing mountains and crossing rivers as he made his way into the United States, learning English and Braille within an indifferent school system, advocating for both disability rights and immigration justice in the halls of Congress and at the Illinois Capitol building, training and inspiring other disabled consumers, all the while beating a path to law school, I realized that I was sitting across from The Man without Fear. This Dreamer, who came of age under the nurturing and empowering wing of the Progress Center, was already a superhero. Matt Murdoch received heightened super-senses from the radiation; Gerardo Salinas's life journey gave him a heightened sense of injustice. Today, maybe this is the kind of superhero we need most.

Civics Lab with Professor Larry

The train conductor looked up and down the rail car, eyes searching for someone with authority among the blind passengers, people in wheelchairs, and the African American and Hispanic personal assistants. No, they wouldn't have the tickets, he reasoned. A man in a wheelchair flailed about and made unintelligible noises. "Who's got the tickets for this group?" the conductor asked, in his booming "conductor voice." The flailing man in the wheelchair became more agitated. The conductor approached me, the apparently abled white man.

"Do you have the tickets?" he asked. "No," I replied. "Larry, the gentleman trying to get your attention, has them." With the help of a personal assistant (PA), advocacy coordinator Larry Biondi produced the tickets. Welcome to Larry's World.

Larry has cerebral palsy, a nonprogressive disability affecting muscle control, balance, and in Larry's case, speech. It often appears to onlookers as something else, a kind of severe developmental disability, what in another time would be called mental retardation. When Larry was born in 1964, doctors told his parents, "The only advice I can give you is to put him in a nursing home. He is going to be like a vegetable. He's not going to be able to do much. His cerebral palsy is very severe; it affects everything."

But Larry's parents soon understood he was a very bright boy—a very bright boy with cerebral palsy. Larry's speech, though difficult to understand at first, became intelligible over time. The Biondis' understanding of their only child's potential and Larry's tenacious commitment to shattering barriers produced a man who now helps other disabled people overcome obstacles—both those self-imposed and those enforced by society. At one point early in his life, doctors told Larry he would never ride a bicycle. His response: logging five thousand miles on a tricycle. Today, Larry would take on new barriers, assisted by community organizing advocate Clark, three Progress Center legislative advocacy interns, and seven other Progress Center members, including Henry.

When the train reached Springfield, Larry led the Progress Center leaders, with assistance, through a brief orientation. We walked, rolled, and scooted our way almost a mile to the Capitol building, across cracked sidewalks and potholed streets. The "curb cuts" and street crossing mats appeared flawless, but as anyone in a wheelchair knows, accessibility is more than curb cuts. I watched as wheelchair-bound leaders dodged the ruts in the road and expertly guided their chairs through what seemed like an obstacle course.

Moving up a long entrance ramp and into the Capitol building, we split up into five groups of three; I was embedded with Larry, Clark, and Henry, accompanied by Larry's PA. Each group prepared to visit their own representatives and senators, based on their legislative districts. Each, in turn, presented Progress Center's perspective on a proposed progressive tax increase to their representative and senator.

Like many states, Illinois faced massive budget deficits following the Great Recession. In response, legislators passed a temporary tax increase in 2011: from a flat 3.75 percent to 5 percent. The tax increase would expire in January 2015. Progress Center and its allies proposed that the tax drop to 2.9 percent for the first $12,500 of income, then rise to 4.9 percent for income from $12,500 to $180,000, with all income above $180,000 taxed at 6.9 percent. For Progress Center members, the logic was simple: people living in poverty should pay less in taxes; people living well should pay higher rates. If the legislature passed no tax increase at all, cuts to services for the disabled were expected.

We entered Rep. Camille Lilly's (D) office. Rep. Lilly represents the Seventy-Eighth District, Henry's neighborhood in Oak Park, as well as neighborhoods in Chicago. She was "on the Floor" debating some of the very issues Henry wanted to discuss. He spoke about the tax issue to a remarkably attentive and engaged receptionist, the first person to treat our group with respect all day. Henry motored out of the office feeling disappointed, but heard.

We forged on, through several offices on Larry's list, wading through a tide of lobbyists and constituents representing varied interests. As advocacy director, Larry targeted several representatives and senators for whom we brought no constituents. In every office, it was the same story: polite reception, respectful hearing (Larry uses his speech machine), but no elected official. Finally, Larry announced a change in strategy: "We're going to them. Let's go to the Floor!"

It was a busy day at the Capitol. Among the smaller bands of lobbyists and interest groups, two other organizations were out in force. A charter schools lobby turned out scores of teachers, and the Community Renewal Society, a "progressive, faith-based organization" working on issues like housing, jobs, and criminal justice, numbered several hundred attendees. As we crossed through a crowded second-floor mezzanine to just outside the House chambers, I feared the sea of activists would not part for the two wheelchairs and one scooter. But they did, and we quickly set up camp at the security gate. Any representative leaving the floor would have to pass by Larry, who was parked closest to the door.

Larry submitted business cards with the names of the representatives, requesting they come outside for a brief meeting. A few of them did. Henry hung back, but watched each person exiting. Then he saw her. "Ms. Lilly!" he called. "I need a word with you."

She recognized Henry and walked up, shaking his hand. Henry started the conversation on the subject of accountability, noting her promise to meet with disabled constituents at the Progress Center. She had not yet scheduled that meeting. Rep. Lilly apologized and promised to reschedule. Henry explained Progress Center's position on making Illinois income taxes progressive, and she noted her support. They shook hands. Henry was ecstatic: "I kept praying, 'Holy Ghost help me!' And He did!"

Henry confessed he had begun to wonder if the long journey to Springfield was worth it. But the in-person encounter with his representative, her renewed commitment to meet with other disabled constituents, and pledge of support for the tax initiative made it all worthwhile—the waiting, patiently watching for the right moment to approach. On the train ride home, Bruce shared a similar story of patience rewarded. He never spoke directly to his representative or senator, but felt respected by the staff who listened to him. With so many science labs behind him, Bruce now found himself learning in Professor Larry's civics lab, studying the interaction of powers in public life instead of ciphering force vectors in the physical realm.

Bruce predicted the disability rights movement would reach its greatest heights when conventional wisdom recognizes that we are all disabled. "Some people don't realize that, or don't want to, because of the label." Despite the loss of some sight, Bruce has found new power in disability rights advocacy. Power enough to displace any internalized stigma. "I'm not perfect," he said, "but they seem to feel I can contribute somehow. That's key, to have that sense that somebody believes that you could do something important."

Beyond Empowerment

Bruce's embracing of a disabled identity also empowered him. Paul's message to the Church at Corinth seems especially prescient: "For whenever I am weak, then I am strong" (2 Cor. 12:10). For Bruce and so many of the leaders I met at the Progress Center, power came only after they accepted their frailty, never before. A piece of artwork gracing the walls of the Progress Center illustrates this idea.

A framed oil painting by Artemio Garcia arrests the eye at the Progress Center's Blue Island Satellite Office. Lady Liberty sits in a wheelchair, torch aloft. Even as she sits, it's not a position of repose. She appears to be straining to lift the torch even higher. Artemio painted this image holding a paintbrush by mouth, his own wheelchair parked close by.

In 1992, at age eighteen, Artemio immigrated to the United States, without authorization. Six months after he arrived, he walked into a convenience store robbery gone bad and took a bullet to the neck, damaging his spinal cord irreparably. Artemio would never use his arms or legs again. A Native American of the Oaxaca region of Mexico, he didn't even speak Spanish, let alone English. Artemio was placed in Oak Forest Hospital of Cook County, where he learned to paint, operating the brush with his mouth. In 2006, Cook County Commissioner Bob Simon ordered the deportation of any unauthorized immigrants in the long-term care facility as a means of cost cutting.

The move alarmed both the disability community and politically active Latinos. Artemio organized a group of protestors within the hospital. The Progress Center sent leaders to protests throughout Cook County. County Commissioner Robert Maldonado took up the cause and became the bearer of Progress Center leaders' stories to fellow commissioners.

Some commissioners expressed concern about the strain on county finances. Quadraplegics like Artemio brought no money into public hospitals from private health insurance, Social Security, or Medicaid. Horacio recalled saying to Cook County President Todd Stroger, "Well, if you fly them back, they are going to die right away. Because they are not going to get the services we have here."

The county commissioners voted to allocate $3 million for three years to assist thirty undocumented migrants in local nursing homes, including Artemio. Shortly afterwards, he began landing contracts for artwork—postcards and paintings for corporate offices. He married, lives independently with his new wife, and is now on track to become a citizen of the United States. To thank Progress Center, whose intervention made the difference between the life he now has and certain death, he painted Lady Liberty in a wheelchair.

Staring at the painting, I saw Henry, Horacio, Loree, Gerardo, Larry, Anne, Bruce, Clark, and all of the other Progress Center leaders and staff. As we hear their stories, we cannot reduce them to labels like "empowered disability rights activists." Their contribution is far greater. They *are* Lady Liberty. Each leader, with her or his uniquely American story, represents a larger struggle to achieve a fully American life, to reach that full potential called for both in Catholic teaching on Integral Human Development and in the Declaration of Independence: "Life, liberty, and the pursuit of happiness."

A thousand miles away, just southwest of Tucson, a community of Native Americans, the Tohono O'odham Nation, might ask if they were ever meant to be included in that declaration.

Tohono O'odham Community Action (TOCA), the next stop on our pilgrimage, empowers this community of "the people of the desert" to assert their autonomy as a sovereign nation in fighting obesity and diabetes by returning to traditional foods, produced locally. Central to their efforts, TOCA promotes the adoption of O'odham *lifeways*, a set of cultural touchstones that illuminate a path out of poverty and disease.

Chapter 5

The Power of *Himdag*:
Tohono O'odham Community Action

In fidelity to the Gospel, and in response to the urgent needs of the present time, we are called to reach out to those who find themselves in the existential peripheries of our societies and to show particular solidarity with the most vulnerable of our brothers and sisters.

—Pope Francis
Message on the Occasion of the Assembly of the
World Council of Churches, October 4, 2013

Cissimarie Juan stood alongside Topawa Road, deep in the heart of Arizona's Tohono O'odham (pronounced *TOE know ODD thuhm*) Nation, just southwest of Tucson, well beyond the physical, as well as existential, peripheries of our society. She surveyed her childhood neighborhood, lingering at the yard where she met Tohono O'odham Community Action (TOCA) cofounder Tristan Reader sixteen years earlier. Long before ten childhood friends went to prison or died, before TOCA began fighting diabetes and the exploitation of basket weavers, before she came to work with the organization as a youth leadership developer, even prior to joining TOCA's first basket-weaving class at age eight, she struck up a conversation with a stranger working his garden.

Cissiemarie recounts her journey with TOCA at Desert Rain Café.

"We saw Tristan planting in his garden," she recalled. "He was not O'odham, so we were curious. Kids were asking, 'Who is this guy and what is he doing?' I got some courage to go meet him and asked him, 'What are you doing?'"

"He told us, 'I'm planting! I'm gardening!' At the time, I had never made the connection that my food comes from the ground. He taught me that. I remember he was growing mint, and he took a piece and handed it to me saying, 'Here, taste this.' I put it in my mouth, and I was so amazed at how much it tasted like gum."

Cissimarie continued to visit Tristan's garden, helping in ways she could. His wife Karen Wyndham, now TOCA's development director, was pastor of Papago United Presbyterian Church, and made the parsonage and other church properties available for community use. When Tristan met award-winning basket weaver Terrol Dew Johnson, they began talking about the challenges facing the O'odham: poverty, unemployment, drugs, diabetes. After many late-night conversations, they decided to create an organization to fight back with the weapons they knew best—

basket weaving and agriculture. And they invited Cissimarie to attend their initial basket weaving class.

"So, at the age of eight, Terrol taught me to make my first basket," she said. "I learned that there were so many ways to hurt myself! The tools for basket weaving are very sharp. I remember when I would poke myself and everyone would say 'OW!' or make an expression. Terrol would always say, 'You better get used to it—this is something you're going to be doing the rest of your life.' So every time now when someone has that experience, that's exactly what I say to them. You've got to get used to it!"

Cissimarie joined the basket weaving classes, and then participated in the first *Bahidaj* (pronounced *BY daj*) cactus harvest camps and TOCA youth groups before becoming a TOCA youth organizer herself. As a young adult in 2006, she fulfilled a lifelong dream of winning the Miss Tohono O'odham pageant, the judges honoring her basket weaving and youth work with TOCA. To her surprise, she then won the Miss Indian Arizona pageant and placed in the top third of contestants in the Miss Indian World pageant. Unlike mainstream beauty contests, tribal pageants are not judged primarily on physical beauty but instead focus on cultural knowledge, traditional skills, and community service.

At each pageant, Cissimarie drew attention to TOCA's youth outreach, fighting gang life, poverty, and hopelessness with the power of O'odham *himdag,* or lifeways. The various awards facilitated travel throughout Arizona and the southwest, but TOCA is now taking Cissimarie places she never thought she would ever see: Paris, France, and Torino, Italy, in 2012, where she shared the O'odham staples of brown and white tepary beans at the Global Food Market Place and the *Internationale Salone del Gusto.* As TOCA's outreach coordinator, she works to share the O'odham *himdag* outside the reservation, even on other continents.

"Who would I be and where I would be without this organization?" Cissimarie often asks. "Because a lot of the kids I grew up with and who were with me when we went to see Tristan and learn about what he was doing, a lot of them are deceased, because of gang activity and health issues, and some of them are in prison. There were at least ten who died or went to prison—most of my friends at the time."

On the day of our interview, Cissimarie was responsible for outreach to forty representatives of other Native American tribes who came to the Tohono O'odham Nation for a preconference, immediately prior to the 2013 Celebration of Basketry and Native Foods. They attended to learn how they might reach back into their own traditions for tools to fight poverty and diabetes and help at-risk youth. Feeling the pull of her conference duties, Cissimarie took one last look at the old garden site, and we piled back into her car.

The Challenge: Poverty, Obesity, and Diabetes

"We thought smallpox was bad!" a conference speaker from another tribe cracked, the anger in her voice crowding out any semblance of humor. What that disease was to the colonial period, warfare against white encroachment to the nineteenth century, and alcoholism to the twentieth, obesity and diabetes are to twenty-first-century Native American life, particularly on reservations where poverty is concentrated. Nationally, 40.8 percent of Native Americans are obese; 17.5 percent have Type II Diabetes. That compares to rates of 26.2 percent for obesity and a 7.6 percent prevalence of diabetes among U.S. non-Hispanic whites.[1]

Among the 22,000 Tohono O'odham who live on the main reservation (over two-thirds of the tribe), an area of the Sonora Desert near Tucson larger than Connecticut, the Indian Health Service (IHS) estimates the incidence of Type II diabetes to be over 50 percent, based on a National Institutes for Health (NIH) study of the O'odham and nearby Pima tribes.[2] These are the highest rates of diabetes on the planet. Among Tohono O'odham children, a 2010 measurement of Body Mass Index (BMI) by local IHS staff found that 76 percent of eleven- to thirteen-year-olds have BMI above the eighty-fifth percentile and are chronically overweight or obese. Given these numbers, the IHS staff anticipates that three-quarters of all Tohono O'odham children born after 2002 will eventually develop Type-II diabetes.[3]

In addition, within the reservation, 41 percent live in poverty, and over 50 percent of households with children live below poverty level.[4] Fully 92 percent of children living in the Tohono O'odham Nation qualify for free or reduced-cost school meals.[5] With poverty statistics like these, school lunch and breakfast programs have become the mainstay of child nutrition within the Tohono O'odham nation. Early on, the first TOCA leaders who researched these programs discovered that the foundation of the meals provided was, simply put, a heap of sugar. On a school cafeteria tour, they saw the day's breakfast: pancakes with syrup, fruit cocktail in syrup, and chocolate milk. "Sugar upon sugar, upon sugar," Tristan described.

If, as many nutritional scientists suggest, Native Americans, in general, and the Tohono O'odham, in particular, have a genetic predisposition to diabetes, this government-sponsored menu is nothing short of a box of smallpox blankets, however well intentioned. Scientists suggest that ten thousand years of foraging, hunting, and farming in the desert switched various O'odham genes for metabolism on and off until their bodies became particularly efficient at turning calories into fat. As a cactus conserves water, their bodies conserve fat, which worked well as long as they consumed traditional high-fiber, slow-digesting foods, like tepary beans, prickly pear, and *ciolim* (pronounced *CHO luhm*, cactus buds).[6]

For thousands of years, Type II diabetes (the disease most associated with obesity) was unheard of among the Tohono O'odham. But as O'odham men returned from World War II, they left their farm implements in the fields (some are still there!) and took jobs with cotton producers near the reservation. In the 1930s, the Tohono O'odham were 100 percent food self-sufficient, producing many traditional crops, cultivated in about twenty thousand acres in the floodplain of the Sonoran lowlands. By 1949, only about 2,500 acres continued to be farmed. By 2000, that number had fallen to two hundred. The O'odham had become nearly 100 percent food dependent and were eating foods known to damage their health. In a few short years, the O'odham shifted from producing all of their food (including 1.8 million pounds of tepary beans) to producing almost nothing (less than 100 pounds).[7] Families began to center their diets around highly processed foods purchased at stores with the men's wages and processed commodity foods paid for by the U.S. government and distributed through various social welfare programs.

Herein lies the structural problem. It might be easy to ask an individual with diabetes, "Why don't you eat better?" but if the school breakfast and lunch programs are spiked with liters of high-fructose corn syrup and the only grocery store on the reservation sells almost exclusively processed food, popovers, and frybread (a twentieth-century pan-tribal treat akin to beignets or funnel cakes), one begins to realize the futility of that question. God created the Sonora Desert, but, through decisions that may have been well intentioned at one time, our society has turned it into a "food desert"—a place where fresh fruits, vegetables, and other whole foods are nearly impossible to find, and highly processed, high salt, high sugar meals are inescapable.

There is much discussion today of the sovereignty of Native American nations like the Tohono O'odham. Under U.S. law, nations like the Tohono O'odham are "domestic dependent nations," and do not share all of the independence of foreign nations, but in many matters, their own governments rule. But how sovereign is the nation if it is entirely dependent on outsiders for its food supply? By the same token, if a large portion of its population is unemployed and dependent on outside welfare programs, how sovereign is that nation?

Unemployment stands at 35.5 percent on the Tohono O'odham Sells Reservation (named after its capital), compared to 9.5 percent overall within the state of Arizona. Of those employed in the formal economy, three-fourths hold public sector positions.[8] These positions usually come with inflexible educational and criminal records requirements, disqualifying many of the unemployed. They will typically then make do with various odd jobs and microenterprises, ranging from operating food trucks to drug trafficking.

In the mid-1990s, Terrol observed many basket weavers supplementing their income through the sale of handicrafts, but they were exploited by outside traders who offered minimal payment, then steeply marked prices up for resale. He offered a common story:

> One elderly weaver had made a harvest basket, which depicts the Saguaro (cactus) harvest. Right before Christmas, this weaver caught a ride to Sells, to see if this trader could buy her basket. She said she had been waiting and waiting for him. He always came before Christmas, but didn't come that year. So we asked, "How much do you want for it?" She said, "Well, he always gives me a hundred dollars for it." A basket like that would retail for $1,300 or more. We said, "We can't give you less than $700 for it," and she just broke down crying, saying, "All these years I've been selling to him like that."

As the number of these stories only increased, and youth gang activity continued to grow, Terrol and Tristan felt called to create an organization to help the community fight back, utilizing the lifeways of O'odham culture, or *himdag*. Tristan described a pivotal moment:

> At the end of the summer, when we started the basket weaving classes, a big gang fight started behind the church. Three kids were stabbed, and two of them were airlifted into Tucson. This other kid from the neighborhood came to us right after that summer program. He said, "Hey, are you going to start to do stuff after school? Because I have

to start to make choices!" He literally put it out there for us. It was that clear to him—that he was going to have to choose which way to go with things.

Shortly afterwards, Terrol returned from a pan-tribal gathering of basket weavers in California with the notion of starting a basketry association in the Tohono O'odham Nation. No support from the tribal government was forthcoming, but Terrol and Tristan nevertheless raised enough donations and grant money, including $15,000 from the Catholic Campaign for Human Development (CCHD), to launch TOCA.

Tristan and Terrol continued to listen to young people, parents, elders, and other informal community leaders throughout TOCA's first years. Conversation after conversation yielded the same themes: the need for cultural revitalization, economic development, the rebuilding of food systems, empowerment of youth, and the promotion of health and wellness among all of the Tohono O'odham. These program areas continue to take center stage.

These two men started TOCA doing what they knew—Terrol teaching basket weaving and Tristan training children how to garden, raising traditional O'odham foods, and harvesting the fruits of the desert plants like the ubiquitous Saguaro (armed) cactus. As these efforts gained in popularity, programs grew, spinning off new ideas and incorporating youth leaders into the staff and board. Today, TOCA comprises several program areas, united by the organization's mission, like a wheel supported by spokes.

The Wheel of TOCA

The Man in the Maze

If you browse TOCA's Desert Rain Gallery, located a short hallway from its offices and award-winning Desert Rain Café, you will begin to recognize a familiar image: "The Man in the Maze." The figure of a man stands partly entered into a labyrinth. He is *l'Itoi* (pronounced *EE toy*), Creator of all living things on the earth, humanity's "elder brother." The labyrinth is, according to the Tohono O'odham, the map to *l'Itoi's* house. The path begins with long gentle arcs and predictable turns, but it ends with surprise twists as we get closer to the end of our journey and return to the Creator.

"The Man in the Maze" is the most popular design found at TOCA's Desert Rain Gallery, an integral component of the organization's logo, fashioned inside the "O" in TOCA. As I interviewed TOCA leaders, toured one of their farms, and met their farmers, gardeners, educators, and basket weavers, it was not hard to understand why The Man in the Maze is fundamental. All Tohono O'odham enter the maze; each must find their way. But TOCA provides a cultural compass: the O'odham *himdag*, a set of lifeways (foods, legends, songs, games, language) to navigate one's way through the maze of life. TOCA also provides friends and partners for the journey through each of its main programs: Project *Oidag* (pronounced *OY dog*), the New Generation of O'odham Farmers, the Desert Rain Café, school programs, Desert Rain Gallery, publications, and conferences.

Project Oidag

When cousins Jesse Juan and Ju:ki (pronounced *JUKE*) Patricio finished high school, their employment options were few: short-term jobs here, helping out relatives there. Nothing steady and nothing leading to advancement. Then they heard about TOCA's youth internship, Project *Oidag* (O'odham word for field, farm, or garden), which offered training in gardening; education about O'odham traditional stories, songs, and games; and opportunities to educate children and youth about healthy eating.

Their pride in the *Oidag* shone as we toured the garden, located on the site of the IHS hospital in Sells. The first feature one notices is its shape, made up of clusters of circle beds: thin at one end, round and wide at the middle, and thin again at the outer end, like a turtle, in honor of a traditional O'odham story.

The power of O'odham stories is not lost on these two young men. As they point out various crops in the garden, Jesse begins to describe one his favorite legends:

> Long ago, we lived at a time of abundant meat—we had plenty of javelinas (hogs), deer, and quail. We developed a taste for meat. So we started eating more and more meat, and then *l'Itoi*, the Creator, got mad, and took all the animals and hid them away. Later on in the story, Coyote [a mischievous creature who appears in many O'odham stories] sets them free.
>
> After that, this boy who was trying to learn how to hunt went out with his grandfather, who was always kind of mean to him. The boy went into the forest and shot a deer, with his bow and arrow. He wounded it, but he couldn't catch it, so he wound up just letting it go.
>
> So later on that night, he told his grandfather, and his grandfather scolded him. He ordered him, "You go out and find that deer!" So he went out and found it. He came to a cave where he thought the deer had been and he went inside the cave. He was lost for four days and four nights before he actually saw the people who were in the cave. They blamed him for this man who was wounded. So they kept him for a year.
>
> Later on, the boy came out of the cave and he saw all of these people turn into deer. So they ran out and he tried to go to his village, and as he went out, he turned into a deer himself. Then the people in the village tried to hunt him. So he ran back to the cave. The deer people said, "We're going to let you go, but you're not allowed to hunt anymore." So they let him go and that's how *Oidagum* (gardening) got started.

Jesse explained that the story's message is not vegetarianism, but balance. The lesson of the deer people came only after the

O'odham began relying too much on meat. "The wintertime is the time to rely on hunting," he continued. "The summer is the time for planting." This story, and others we discussed, clearly had significant meaning for Jesse. Agriculture was a new world, and the stories and songs he learned helped him personally connect to traditional values and the cycles of planting and harvesting, watering and cultivating.

Ju:ki, on the other hand, grew up helping in his mother's garden. He thought gardening was a "woman's thing," but he liked planting, even though it felt strange to be tending the only garden in his village. When his family moved to Sells, he signed up for a fifteen-month TOCA youth internship. A dozen youth aged fourteen to twenty-five participated, learning about O'odham foods; traditional stories and songs; and games like *songiwul* (pronounced *SON wool*), a race with a wooden kickball for men, and *toka* (pronounced *TOE ka*), a sport akin to field hockey and played with saguaro cactus ribs as sticks. The interns also helped out with TOCA school programs. They earned a $500 per month stipend for fifteen months for their participation, working even when TOCA could not pay them while the U.S. Farm Bill languished in Congress.

The songs and stories brought gardening to life for the interns. Ju:ki even gained a newfound appreciation for his nickname, which means "rain." When the internship period ended, participants asked if the program could be extended, a development TOCA staff welcomed. A Friday graduation ceremony concluded the internship, and then a funny thing happened. Ju:ki and half of his group showed up for work on Monday. TOCA staff huddled quickly, and Ju:ki found himself one of the first leaders of Project *Oidag*, a second-level internship, paying the same $500/month stipend. Cousin Jesse, familiar with TOCA from a summer job at TOCA's original teaching farm, Papago Farms, signed up for the first group of Project *Oidag* interns as well.

As Ju:ki and Jesse reflected on their Project *Oidag* experience, they displayed an interest in growing produce, but an even greater passion for the cultural dimensions of traditional O'odham farming, learning concepts like *s-wa:gima* (pronounced *SWAG eh meh*), which means "to be industrious or hardworking." The songs and stories, prayers and blessings, and even the traditional games helped them reclaim a part of their heritage in danger of being lost. "This helped me realize who I am," Ju:ki said.

Project *Oidag* has endeared the *Oidag* gardeners to their grandparents, the O'odham elders, who recall a time when the Tohono O'odham Nation produced much of its own food and now play a vital role in TOCA, teaching youth and young adults how to prepare the traditional foods. Jesse explained,

> After I started, my grandfather would tell me stories about how his grandfather used to manage the fields out in our village—then we would drive from one end of the village to the other, talking about where all the old fields used to be. Because that's how the village got its name—"Big Fields." Each family had their own fields that they managed. It's pretty cool to be able to talk to him, and they are pretty excited to hear that we're trying to get the youth back into it. That's where it all lies, with them.

As Jesse spoke about O'odham youth, he stood tall, adult features formed, with a strength and maturity in his voice. Through TOCA, *he* was now stepping into the role of elder, following the example of his grandparents.

Today, parents are supportive of their children's involvement with TOCA. But, as Jesse shared, the people who are *really* impressed are the grandparents. A certain quality of imagination is shared by the oldest and the youngest. Cissimarie explained, "Something unique is going on between youth and elders. Elders understand a lot of what young people are doing. A lot of adults say, 'You can't do that! You don't know what you want. You're not going about it in the right way.' But when it comes to elders, they love that you're at least trying. And they're willing to share more knowledge with you and try to help you."

As their internship enters its final months, Jesse still plans to attend college, but Ju:ki is undecided about the future. The eighteen-month Next Generation of Farmers apprenticeship would be the next step within TOCA, which they are both considering. "We've been getting offers!" Ju:ki noted, with a grin. Perhaps, once again, he will show up for work after *this* internship ends.

New Generation of O'odham Farmers

Sterling Johnson cocked his head and pointed to the reason he became a farmer. "You see that? That's where the bull stepped on my ear," he explained. A rising rodeo star, Sterling grew tired of the ups and downs of the circuit, not to mention the injuries. His winnings from bull riding never fully paid the bills. A series of temporary jobs in demolition and road construction helped, but like rodeo, he couldn't count on the income. Now approaching his thirties, Sterling sought training in work that would provide more dependable income. He settled on farming.

Eager for training, Sterling entered TOCA's New Generation of O'odham Farmers program. There he met Noland Johnson, one of Terrol's younger brothers (and no relation to Sterling), who now manages TOCA's Sells Reservation teaching farm in Cowlic, Arizona. Noland came to farming in his thirties by way of his widowed grandmother. Fifteen years ago, he noticed her increasing frailty and looked for a way to spend more time with her in Cowlic. He helped out here and there for a couple of years, providing some care, until Terrol approached him with an interesting proposition: they could turn the largely dormant family property into a TOCA teaching farm, with Noland as manager. Tohono O'odham elders and local high school agroscience teachers would mentor Noland in some of the finer points of farming, and he would, in turn, mentor new O'odham farmers. The produce would land in various TOCA projects.

The idea appealed to Noland, who had been involved with TOCA since its inception. Watching his four brothers struggle with diabetes gave him passion for growing traditional crops.

Conversations with Mikey Enis, TOCA's school coordinator, gave him an appreciation for the songs, stories, and blessings that made farming not so much a chore, but a fulfillment of his responsibility to work with the Creator. They decided to open Cowlic Farm as an educational center.

As Noland immersed himself in the work of mentoring farmers, a change began to set in. He recalled, "I'm more patient now. I can step back and let ideas flow. I'm not yelling like I used to. I'm also more outspoken. In school, I was the quiet kid in the back. Now I'm on the district council for the area around Cowlic and serve on several committees."

"The quiet kid in the back" became Sterling's professor for the eighteen-month internship. Together with shop technician and mechanic Vernal Sam and fellow apprentice Jesse Garcia, they took on all of the year's farming tasks with a view toward education. Sterling had ranching experience, which helped a little. He was familiar with step-by-step processes like "setting up a horse." But when it came to plants, it was all new territory. "I didn't even know we had beans," he said, referring to the brown and white tepary beans that were staples of the Tohono O'odham prereservation diet. "I didn't know much about farming. I just knew I'd have to work hard."

Sterling noted that a big part of the internship was learning the equipment, mastering the tractor with all of its implements—the tiller, the planter, and more. Coming to terms with the reality of farming in the desert and the paucity of rainfall came later. If they planted at the right times and used a simple irrigation system at key moments, the desert plants would do the rest—thriving where no other crops could.

But Sterling's development did not end there. After a few months he came to view his internship less as a job than a "sacred practice." He took to burning greasewood, which according to O'odham legends is the first plant *l'Itoi* created, to cleanse the land before working the fields, saying a blessing before tilling and praying to the Creator to protect the crops. He also began to take better care of his body and relationships, achieving a purer mind-set as he approached his work. "You have to be pure of mind and let go of whatever might be blocking you, so you can focus that energy within you on prayer," he said.

Like other TOCA leaders, Sterling now believes O'odham physical health will be renewed by returning to the traditional desert foods, but true prosperity will never come without recovering the other dimensions of *himdag*. "Yes, we can grow the food, and that's important. But just as important, we've got to teach why we value the food through the stories and legends about why these foods were given to us."

TOCA's Anthony Francisco, who serves as Cowlic Farm learning coordinator, elaborated on this theme:

> It might seem that we're trying to "turn back the clock," but we're just bringing those values forward. Some things are very healthy to bring back—for example, the food grown in the desert. These foods have sustained us for so many generations, but they also have important cultural significance. There are songs that are sung when a seed is planted. There are songs that are sung when we harvest. There are songs that are sung to help call the rains to make the crops grow and prosper. Although it doesn't seem like we have a lot of control over some of these things at times, when we begin to value our culture, we get that sense of hope that things can get better as a community. So we bring those things forward, with the food, the *himdag*, the way of life, living the best life we can.

TOCA's executive program director, Nina Sajovec Altshul, a Slovenian expert on arid lands agriculture and permaculture, and a doctoral candidate in cultural anthropology, also noted the importance of food in the Oodham *himdag*. "Plants embody not just the character of the land, but also the people, and vice versa. There are all the things that come from the tepary bean, from planting it, to growing it, to harvesting it, to sharing it," she explained. "You cook them a longer time, over an open flame, to get the traditional taste of it. Now, that's time you spend with your family. That's time you spend with other women. It's time the men spend collecting the wood for the fire. It's the time spent planting, with all of those planting songs."

The O'odham *himdag,* Anthony continued, is not meant to be hoarded, but shared. Sharing is another ten-thousand-year-old O'odham tradition, essential for survival in an unforgiving desert clime. In today's information society, he explained, we need to be attentive to sharing ideas and wisdom as well as food from the earth.

O'odham squash, tepary beans, *l'Itoi's* onions, all fruits of the farm: where do they go? Much of the produce is used at the Desert Rain Café, TOCA's Zagat-rated restaurant, spreading the message through the language of cooking. Dried beans and dried desert-harvested foods, like cholla buds, are sold from the Desert Rain Gallery as packaged goods under TOCA's label, "Tohono O'odham Trading Company." Local schools are increasing their locally sourced ingredients, and TOCA has started Desert Rain Food Service to help local school districts increase and maintain the number of fresh, local, "from scratch" meals served to students. About 15 percent of the tepary beans are sold to restaurants in Arizona where "native cuisine" and "local foods" dominate the menu.

Desert Rain Café

Brian Hendricks, manager of the Desert Rain Café, waved to a new customer entering TOCA's native foods café in Sells' lone strip mall, the only one you'll find for sixty miles in any direction. "Are you the one who does the bad food or the good food?" she asked. "The good food!" he said with a smile. "Try a sample."

Brian knew that the Desert Rain Café sold more than good food—it was a gateway to O'odham *himdag.* Four years ago, when he took a position at the café as a dishwasher, it was just a job. But in a short time, he became curious about the food, farming, and TOCA's message of health and wellness. He began to eat more traditional foods and joined a TOCA running group. "I don't know how much weight I lost," he recalled, "but I went from a size 4X to a size 2X in a year and a half." Health improved and feeling optimistic about the future, Brian gained energy and focus. Clearly growing as a leader, Brian was promoted to manager after a year of washing dishes.

I met Brian in a TOCA conference room within a cluster of offices behind the café shortly after lunch. "Did you try the white tepary bean hummus?" he asked, referencing a new twist on an O'odham staple. "Yes," I reply, "Best I ever had," and I notice how good I feel, as the high-fiber tepary beans slow down the usual blood-sugar spike after a high-carb meal. "How about the pico de gallo with ciolim (pronounced *CHORE-lum*)?" he inquired, regarding a salsa made with wild cactus buds high in calcium. "Great—I wish I could take a bottle home with me," I said. "And the grilled chicken with prickly-pear glaze? The squash enchiladas?" "My daughter loved them!"

With that joyful discussion of "good food," we continued our interview. Since 2002, opening a native foods café had been one of Terrol's dreams. With the expansion of TOCA farms and the introduction of the New Generation of O'odham Farmers program, TOCA was producing traditional O'odham crops in abundance. The challenge became making these foods affordable and accessible, overcoming the food desert phenomenon with O'odham *himdag*.

To be sure, opening a café in the midst of the Great Recession on an Indian reservation struggling with poverty involved some measure of risk, but nevertheless, the Desert Rain Café opened its doors in 2009. It has since attracted a great deal of attention within the O'odham community but also from "foodies" from Tucson and tourists from all over the world. The café is even featured in the Zagat restaurant guide for Tucson. Sometimes the café's lines snake outside onto the sidewalk, but people patiently stay in queue. Later, many remark, "It's worth the wait."

The Desert Rain Café has become well known in the region. Guest chefs from some of southern Arizona's best "native cuisine" restaurants are invited monthly to cook a special four-course meal at the Desert Rain Café, to bring "fine dining" to the reservation. Native chefs like Nephi Craig and Iron Chef's Ryan Clark have brought their native foods recipes in for special dining experiences.

The café's success led TOCA to set up a catering operation, bringing the Desert Rain Café to events as far as Tucson and Phoenix. This spin-off, and discussions of founding an even larger restaurant in Tucson, show TOCA making progress in its efforts to repair a broken food system, but the next step, TOCA staff believe, is changing the practices of the major institutional food providers. These businesses provide meals for reservation schools, the IHS hospital, and the tribe's Early Childhood Education program (akin to Head Start). The difference in scale is that of feeding thousands vs. feeding hundreds. This dimension is one reason TOCA emphasizes its work with schools.

Bringing *Himdag* to *School Lunch*

Don't tell Mikey Enis (or any other TOCA leader) that children and youth are "the leaders of the future." Here at TOCA, young people are considered leaders of the present. Mikey is TOCA's school foods, culture, and native nutrition program coordinator. As a child, he came up through Terrol's basket weaving classes and took an interest in basketry and rattle making, but most of all, it was the singing workshops that caught his attention. Whenever he had a chance, Mikey tried to learn what he could about the songs and stories that moved his heart growing up.

Mikey spent as much time as he could with Tohono O'odham elder Danny Lopez (1937–2008), a teacher, singer, and storyteller who devoted his life to passing on tribal culture to young people. A student of linguistics, Lopez taught the Tohono O'odham language, songs, stories, games, and diet in any venue he could find, once walking 250 miles to give a presentation. Lopez was also a key inspiration to TOCA, leading many activities during its first decade and serving on its staff early on. Mikey is one of several of Danny Lopez's students who now pass those traditions on to their peers, youth, and children.

Through his position as the Tohono O'odham Nation Youth Council manager (a tribal government post), Mikey met Cissimarie and grew more aware of TOCA's work. When the school coordinator position opened up, Mikey jumped at the chance to become part of the organization. "I admired the idea of preserving the *himdag*," he recalled. "It sustained our ancestors since creation. We *need* to do this!"

Mikey elaborated on traditional songs as essential to the O'odham lifeways. "We as O'odham are always singing," he explained. "We're musical people. In our grandparents' generation, the men were always in the fields, singing, wanting the rain, wanting rain clouds to come, hoping for good crops. Singing made the time go by. Every job, every moment can have a song."

Mikey took a moment to consider a song to share, and decided upon one sung at TOCA's annual summer *Bahidaj* (pronounced BYE-*daj*) Camp, when three hundred O'odham come together for the three-day saguaro harvest. Participants learned how to pick ripe fruit from the iconic multiarmed cactus. They separated the pulp from the seeds to make *sitol* (SEE tall), or syrup. Temperatures sometimes reached 110 degrees, but the group punctuated harvesting with workshops on leadership and O'odham culture.

Mikey began to sing, and this gentle, soft-spoken young man was transformed. His voice rose in volume as if he were singing for three hundred people. The song carried into the Desert Rain Gallery and Café and outside into the desert:

> The red cactus fruit that's growing over there
> Is growing far away,
> And it's standing there against the wall.
> The fruit is all red.
> Even though it's far away, I'm going to go get it.
> The clouds roll over, over in the sky above me.

Mikey finished the song, waited a few beats, and then took pains to make sure I understood that it came from another region of the reservation and was not his original composition. Many O'odham songs, unlike stories, are an individual's creation and not for mass distribution.

Mikey's work in the schools includes teaching songs and stories, but always within an agricultural context. Together with Food Corps volunteers Rebecca Cohen and Julia Munson, he teaches Indian Oasis Elementary School students how to grow traditional O'odham foods like tepary beans, O'odham squash, *l'Itoi* onions, O'odham corn, and O'odham peas, along with broccoli, purple carrots, cauliflower, beets, cilantro, spinach, chard, and kale. The middle school has a similar *Oidag*, and TOCA's high school program includes work with the FFA (Future Farmers of America) and a four-day food justice curriculum. TOCA also sponsors a high school cooking club, which won the 2010 National "Cooking Up Change" competition sponsored by the Healthy Schools Campaign and the National Farm to School Network with its tepary bean quesadilla recipe, now served in reservation schools.

At Indian Oasis Elementary School, Mikey leads the singing of traditional songs while the children work. If they have time, he will introduce an O'odham game. Typically the school harvest also yields a math problem or two, which the children solve in their class. The produce will be served in the school lunch program. At lunchtime, students line up at the "culture bar," bragging to friends that *they* harvested today's lunch.

The culture bar emerged from discussions with the multinational food service provider and the school superintendent about how to integrate traditional O'odham foods into the school lunch program. Today, each meal contains a "Tohono O'odham entrée" option, and several traditional foods in the salad bar. TOCA Project *Oidag* youth interns (the class that refused to leave) created novel cartoon characters to promote the O'odham food—each character representing a different plant, increasing the visibility of the traditional foods. At present, depending on the school, between 30 and 100 percent of students choose the Tohono O'odham entrée.

While these changes to the school lunch program were a step forward (how many schools have the occasional garden-to-table salad bar?), TOCA leaders nevertheless saw the changes as incomplete. Many children at Indian Oasis still eat high-sugar, low-fiber meals, a diet likely to produce diabetes in a majority of O'odham by adulthood.

If we think back to the origins of the school lunch program, such a menu seems counterproductive. The School Lunch Act of 1946 was in many ways a response to the fact that half of the draftees for World War II failed their physicals, mainly due to malnutrition. During the Cold War, Congress and President Truman responded by founding the school lunch program, underscoring the state's interest in raising healthy men and women to serve in the armed forces. Subsequent amendments expanded the reach of the program, adding breakfasts nationwide in 1975. If, like the O'odham, over half the men registering for the draft today were diagnosed with Type II diabetes, what would be the national response?

TOCA is not waiting for a national reform of school lunch programs. With two farms up and running, new farmers in training, the café doing brisk business and drawing increased catering work, TOCA is poised to take the next step—a fully operative food production and distribution system. To that end, TOCA founded Desert Rain Food Services, led by Brooklyn native Stephanie Lip, a Food Corps volunteer who, like so many others, opted to stick around after her term of service ended.

Stephanie is currently working with the Bureau of Indian Education, the local school district, and the Early Childhood Education centers to assess their capacity to cook from scratch using fresh, local ingredients. When up and running, the service aims to provide traditional meals to twelve hundred students daily, integrating the meal services with nutrition and wellness education, school garden activities, and cultural programming, creating living-wage food service jobs and increased demand for traditional foods. With the Early Childhood Education Program signed up as the first client, Mikey will soon have the opportunity to discuss health, well-being, and culture with the preschoolers consuming 100 percent traditional Tohono O'odham breakfasts and lunches.

Desert Rain Gallery and
TOCA Basket Weavers Association

As large as TOCA's food programming has grown, the organization still maintains its roots in basket weaving. Basket-making classes and workshops for young O'odham all the way up to elders continue at multiple venues. But TOCA's most significant contribution in the area of basketry has been stopping the exploitation of basket weavers like Rose Martin.

Rose flashed a shy smile as I approached her table at the 2013 Celebration of Basketry and Native Food Festival, in Tucson's Arizona-Sonora Desert Museum. About twenty O'odham women (and the occasional man) surrounded us, each absorbed in their weaving. About sixty years ago, when Rose was ten, her mother brought her the ends of a white yucca plant and some bear grass and began to teach her to weave. Rose explained that traditionally, a mother or grandmother will begin to teach basket weaving to the girls in the household at age ten or eleven, "when they first become calm."

When I pointed out the different O'odham men I had met that week who seemed good at basket weaving (including Terrol, whose work has been exhibited at the Smithsonian), she laughed and said, "That's the new generation! But my mother told me, it's for the women. Men are supposed to go out and hunt the food." Rose has raised three daughters, teaching each of them the craft, and produced hundreds of baskets.

I watched as she began to weave with bear grass soaked overnight in a wet towel to make it pliable, then split and dried. Rose believes in obtaining all of the materials in the desert herself. "You need to work for it," she said. Once, as Rose gathered bear grass, white yucca, and devil's claw in the desert, she was stopped and questioned by U.S. Border Patrol agents. What on earth could she be doing out there? Rose said she "educated them about basket weaving. They were amazed! They never thought a plant like that could give something back."

Before TOCA founded the Tohono O'odham Basket Weavers Organization (TOBO), Rose used to sell small baskets for $20. Now, she brings in an average of $60 per item, via the Association's Desert Rain Gallery. Weavers get paid 85 percent of a basket's sale price, with 15 percent earmarked for the gallery's rent and management. TOBO launched in 1997 with a $7,500 CCHD startup grant.

Rose works as an official in the tribal courts as her main job, but basket weaving provides needed additional income. Most O'odham basket weavers, including those whose work has been exhibited in museums, cannot support themselves by the craft alone, but TOCA's intervention has helped weaving become a source of supplemental income for basket makers, especially women elders. Some also earn money by teaching the craft to children and youth. Since TOCA/TOBO's inception, baskets and other native artworks have been sold to the tune of $750,000.

Scaling Out

TOCA has begun to see many positive consequences of its efforts, as more O'odham become aware of their *himdag*, participate in community-wide agricultural events, and integrate traditional foods into their diets. But they are not the only tribe examining its relationship to traditional foods. As more Native American communities reclaim their food heritage, for cultural preservation and for health, TOCA has taken on a new role: convener.

When TOCA staff discuss growth, expansion means "scaling out" as much as "scaling up," that is, replicating these models across the country in other Native American nations. Recent awards have raised the organization's national profile. In 2011, TOCA received one of ten global "Imagine There's No Hunger" awards from Why Hunger/Hard Rock Café. Finally, in 2012, cofounder Terrol Dew Johnson was named a White House Food Security "Champion of Change" for his contribution to renewing native foodways.

But TOCA cofounder Tristan Reader doesn't see TOCA going national as much as supporting TOCA-like organizations throughout the United States, "multiplying out across other tribes." To support this pan-tribal vision, TOCA published the first issue of *Native Foodways* magazine in 2013, through funding from the U.S. Department of Agriculture's Office of Outreach and Advocacy for Socially Disadvantaged Farmers. A quarterly, the magazine features articles on various tribes' efforts to preserve traditional foodways and prereservation diets.

In the first two issues, we meet the Muckleshoot people of the Pacific Northwest and learn of their resurgent berry gardens, pick up ways to utilize blue corn from the Hopis, and discover how to forage a delicious desert meal of prickly pear, mescal, banana yucca, and sumac berries from the Hualapai (People of the Tall Pines) of northern Arizona, among other articles. Vendors of native foods like TOCA's Tohono O'odham Trading Company, the Anishinaabe/Ojibwe Native Harvest enterprise, and the Santa Anna Pueblo Company are featured in the issues, so the curious reader can obtain many of the items unavailable in conventional stores.

Profiles of award-winning Native American chefs, several of whom bring traditional foods to tribal casinos, add personal narratives to the metastory of various tribes and their centuries-long relationship to local foods. Additional commentary explains the notion of food sovereignty and provides the nutritional and cultural rationale for adopting prereservation diets. Recipes abound throughout each issue along with "serving suggestion" photography that will make the reader want to try the foods immediately.

Native Foodways editorial director Mary Pagnelli Votto has given us a tool to do just that, along with coauthor Frances Manuel, through their book *From l'Itoi's Garden*. Part cookbook, part ethnobotany lesson, part photo essay, *From l'Itoi's Garden* provides readers with background on many O'odham foods and their place in Tohono O'odham culture. Sections trace the life of the food from planting, to harvesting, to the dinner table, along with songs, stories, and recipes associated with the plants.[9]

Native Foodways and *From l'Itoi's Garden* are two ways TOCA shares efforts to preserve and nurture traditional foodways throughout what some call "Indian country," but nothing beats the power of face-to-face interaction. TOCA therefore has invested in pan-tribal events like the 2013 Celebration of Basketry and Native Food Festival. Here Apaches, Pima, Navajo, Cherokees, and a score of other tribes—some of whom once waged war against each other—come to weave and to share ideas and recipes to reclaim the health that has eluded them since the advent of the "reservation diet."

Reflecting on the diversity of participation at the conference, Mary stated that the conversation about health, wellness, and food sovereignty is now happening "in every Native community at some level." With a view toward "scaling out," TOCA leaders have joined hands with other tribes in a circle of power to overcome poverty and diabetes. Unlike some circles of power, this one faces outward.

Beyond Empowerment

No doubt, TOCA meets most anyone's criteria of an "empowerment organization." If we return to the founders' story, Terrol and Tristan, along with so many O'odham, had watched helplessly as Cissimarie's generation graduated from riding bikes on Topawa Road to gang activity, prison, and early deaths. Until the TOCA founders conceived of responding to these challenges with basket weaving classes and the cultivation of traditional foods, many O'odham lacked "the ability to act." Today, they have the power to respond, but also so much more: they are reclaiming their *himdag.* In addition, the tribe as a whole is inching toward greater sovereignty as the traditional foods portion of the reservation economy grows.

Viewing TOCA through the lens of Integral Human Development, we see attention to more than building power—TOCA brings the O'odham lifeways to bear on all dimensions of life on the reservation. Think of Cissimarie discovering herself as an O'odham woman through basket weaving and traditional songs, then giving back to O'odham youth and now the wider community. Consider Sterling, a bull rider who discovered a deep spirituality in farming, or Brian Hendricks, the dishwasher who dropped two T-shirt sizes and vaulted to manager of the Desert Rain Café. Reflect on Jesse's thoughts on his conversations with his grandfather about farming and the old Big Fields landscape. Each became empowered, but TOCA's emphasis on the O'odham *himdag* developed each person further, offering resources and companions for the twists and turns of life's journey.

When we first arrived at this stop on our pilgrimage, Cissimarie shared the story of losing ten friends to violence, disease, and prison. What would the job prospects of these O'odham be on a reservation already devastated by widespread unemployment? How would a prospective employer view the "Have you ever been convicted of a felony?" box checked "Yes"? The exclusion of people with criminal records from employment is not limited to Native American nations and other places of high unemployment—it reaches into every sector of the U.S. economy. To learn how ex-inmates, particularly recovering addicts, are responding to this form of exclusion from public life, we travel to Worcester, Massachusetts, to meet Ex-Prisoners and Prisoners Organizing for Community Advancement (EPOCA).

Chapter 6

Jobs Not Jails:
Ex-Prisoners and Prisoners
Organizing for Community
Advancement

*God is in everyone's life. Even if the life of a person has been a
disaster, even if it is destroyed by vices, drugs or anything else—
God is in this person's life.*

—Pope Francis
Interview with Jesuit Publications, August 19, 2013

Delia Vega sat with her arms crossed, looking skeptically at
the former prison inmates seated around her in the basement of
a Worcester, Massachusetts, church. "Why did I even come here?"
she asked herself. "They said this meeting was about recovery?! All
anybody is talking about is this thing called CORI and legislators.
I've got to get out of here!"

Someone handed Delia an agenda with the acronym EPOCA
at the top. She began to read, suspiciously. At the top, the key to
the organization's name stood out: "Ex-Prisoners and Prisoners
Organizing for Community Advancement."

Cassandra Bensahih at a Jobs Not Jails rally.

"'Ex-prisoners,'" she thought, "that's me. 'Community Advancement' suggests that folks are trying to do something positive." She began to waver, "Maybe I'll stay and learn more about this organization."

It was time to try something positive. Delia was on the sixth of her "nine lives." She had taken her first drink at thirteen, began using heroin at seventeen, and started smoking crack at eighteen. She was able to avoid brushes with the law for over a decade by asking better-connected friends in Boston to obtain drugs for her. But a move to Springfield, Massachusetts, in her thirties severed those connections, and Delia began to purchase drugs directly from local dealers. Her ability to parent her four children became even more compromised, and the state's Department of Child Protective Services placed her children with their grandparents.

Gang activity also brought out a violent streak. Fights and beatings of women in rival bands of drug dealers became a regular feature of Delia's life. Dangerous situations became an everyday occurrence, and she watched as those "nine lives" counted down. Jumping from a moving car to escape a beating didn't kill her, nor did a spray of bullets that ricocheted off a nearby wall and shattered a bottle at her feet. She had been able to talk down a would-be assassin who had plunged a screwdriver into her neck. It seemed nothing could stop her. Until, in 2006, she almost beat a member of a rival gang to death.

Delia was on the run for two weeks—she thought she had killed the victim. Hidden away, often alone, she began to reflect on her choices. "That's when it hit me," she recalled, "the guilt, the shame, the question, 'What are you doing with your life?'"

Tired of hiding, Delia walked by a police station, where cops quickly recognized and arrested her. "I had such a sense of relief," she said, "when they asked, 'Are you Delia?' and then told me 'You're under arrest for the *assault and battery* of so-and-so.' She wasn't dead! I could deal with that."

Another second chance. How many had she used up already? But this time was different. In court, Delia listened as she was described as a drug addict, a violent menace, a Bad Mom, in short—a monster. "I couldn't believe that the person they were talking about was me," she said. "But I put myself in a situation that gave them that opportunity to talk that way about me, and the actions they described were true."

A judge sentenced Delia to three years in prison. Good behavior at the Massachusetts Correctional Institute (MCI) at Framingham allowed her to serve the last two years on parole. She threw herself into recovery and, later, EPOCA's regimen of 1:1's, strategy meetings, and coalition outreach.

As Delia invested more time organizing citizens returning from prison, she discovered—to her surprise—she was good at it! "Organizing for EPOCA," she recalled, "allowed me to see myself and my capabilities in a whole different way. And I was excited that I was given that opportunity—that people believed in me. For most of my life, nobody even believed that I could change."

In 1:1's and group meetings, again and again, she heard the same story: any conviction amounted to a life sentence of unemployment and difficulty locating housing, and carried additional, seemingly arbitrary "collateral sanctions," punishments piled on top of prison sentences—like a $1,300 fee for drug offenders to reinstate a driver's license after release from prison. This little-known penalty (imposed *after* the inmate had supposedly repaid his or her debt to society) is a surefire guarantee of unemployment in areas of Massachusetts without public transportation.

Delia felt the stigma of incarceration particularly in the areas of parenting and housing. "Mostly it's followed me by preventing me from signing up to be a chaperone at my children's schools," she explained. "I tell my youngest daughter a story to explain why I can't chaperone, because I'm fearful of the aftermath with the teachers at her school if I try. I'm pretty sure they know there's something, because my mom takes care of them, but I don't want them to know the extremes of where I've been. There's supposed to be a process and a conversation, but most people don't know that, and they are just likely to automatically deny you. Because that's the experience of most people I talk to. They say, 'Hey, I can't chaperone at my kid's school. I don't even want to try, because I don't want my children's teachers to see my criminal record or for the school to be aware of it, because I don't want her to have to deal with the aftermath.' It's followed me in the sense that my children are still paying for it."

"I was recently looking for an apartment," she continued. "My husband and I both have criminal records, and we couldn't find a place for a really long time, until we found the apartment that we lived in until recently. It was because we knew the people at the realty office, and they knew the landlord. But he ended up selling the property, and that meant we had to look for another apartment. It was one of the longest searches we ever did, because we were denied based on our criminal records. When we finally got the apartment, it was because I was determined to have a 1:1 conversation with the landlord. I asked 'How long does our daughter have to pay for our mistakes?' We're living in the apartment now."

The Challenge: The Scarlet "X"

In Chapter 2, an ex-inmate in a Seattle Women's Justice Circle said she believed others saw a fluorescent "X" on her person, stigmatizing her as an ex-prisoner and ruling out employment or decent housing. It's not hard to imagine that "X" in a reddish hue, recalling the "A" for *adultery* displayed on Hester Prynne's chest in Nathaniel Hawthorne's classic novel *The Scarlet Letter*.

According to the National Employment Law Project, sixty-five million Americans wear the mark of a conviction,[1] and the U.S. Department of Labor notes that a third of adult U.S. residents have a criminal history that shows up on a background check.[2] It could be an arrest that did not lead to conviction, a conviction with no sentence, or a conviction for a nonviolent crime. Often, among people with a criminal record, jail time was served for low-level drug offenses that might even be legal in other jurisdictions or certainly less harshly punished. Like Delia, these ex-inmates have paid their "debt to society" but soon discover they may neither work again nor find an apartment easily.

Refusing to hire applicants with criminal records has become a de facto means of racial discrimination. Because African Americans account for 28.3 percent of all arrests in the United States while comprising 12.9 percent of the population, ruling out such applicants means ruling out African Americans disproportionately. That is why it is illegal to refuse to hire someone solely on the basis of a criminal record, when that conviction bears no relevance to the job in question.

In 2013, the U.S. Equal Employment Opportunity Commission (EEOC) charged Dollar General and a U.S. division of BMW with dismissing applicants based on criminal background checks "when they should have considered each applicant individually and evaluated whether his or her past arrest or crime had any bearing on the job for which they applied." The EEOC successfully argued that the hiring policies at both companies had the effect of discriminating against black applicants, in violation of Title VII of the 1964 Civil Rights Act, which bars employers from discriminating based on race [among other protected categories including sex and religion]."[3]

Several studies of employer responses to research assistants posing as citizens returning from incarceration illustrate pervasive discrimination against people with criminal records. In an oft-quoted study, researchers found that a criminal record reduces the possibility of a callback or job offer by almost half (28 percent vs. 15 percent). When broken down by race, the results offer further insight. Blacks were three times more likely to suffer a penalty for having a criminal record. Whites received callbacks or job offers 31 percent of the time without criminal records, 22 percent with a criminal record. Blacks received positive responses just 25 percent of the time, even without a criminal record, and 10 percent with one.[4]

In another study of corporations advertising on Craigslist, the National Employment Law Project found several household names like Radio Shack, Domino's Pizza, and Lowe's Home Improvement, among others, flagrantly posting unambiguous bans on applicants with criminal records. These listings included wording like "No Exceptions! . . . No Misdemeanors and/or Felonies of any type ever in background," "DO NOT APPLY WITH ANY MISDEMEANORS/FELONIES," "You must not have any felony or misdemeanor convictions on your record. Period."[5]

The brazenness with which some businesses flout the law on the use of criminal records in background checks inspired returning citizens like Delia (many former prison inmates prefer this term because of its positive emphasis, although not all are citizens of the United States) to begin to organize for reform. In 2009, EPOCA won a unanimous Worcester City Council vote on the use of criminal records in hiring that led, within a year, to a new Massachusetts state law "banning

the box" asking about criminal records on initial job applications. In Worcester, the Fair CORI (Criminal Offender Record
Information) Practices Ordinance "banned the box" from all
applications for employment by any city department or con-
tracting vendor and only allows the question to arise once a
conditional offer of employment has been made. The applicant
then has an opportunity to explain him or herself, after coming
to the point of being selected for a position.

The next year, Massachusetts Governor Deval Patrick signed
into law a bill based on EPOCA's proposal to reform Massachusetts' system governing the dissemination and use of CORI.
Under the new law, both employers and landlords are no longer
allowed to ask, "Have you ever been convicted of a crime?" on
initial applications.

Delia played a key role in the passage of the bill to "ban
the box" in Massachusetts. Months earlier, Massachusetts House
Speaker Robert DeLeo sat on the fence, unsure if the bill should
even come to a vote. Delia attended a meeting with Speaker
DeLeo, as part of the broad coalition allied to reform CORI.
Her assigned role was to explain the merits of one section of the
bill and its contribution to public safety by lowering recidivism
among returning citizens. Another ex-inmate was tapped to tell
his personal story. When the time came for him to speak, he
still had not joined the group in Speaker DeLeo's office. Delia
stepped in and explained how difficult it had been for her family
to obtain an apartment and how intimidating the question on
job applications had been. Speaker DeLeo, who was seated next
to Delia, appeared startled. He leaned in and said, "Well, I never
would have guessed. You seem so smart and articulate!"

"And I was able to say," she continued, "'well, that's exactly
why we need the removal of the criminal record question! So
people can be looked at on their merits and not how they answer
that question. Had I said I was an ex-prisoner before I gave my
presentation, you probably would have blocked your mind com-
pletely'." Speaker DeLeo nodded softly.

Within days, he scheduled a vote, and the CORI reform legislation passed, 138–17. Shortly afterwards, the bill cleared the Senate 26–12 and went on to Governor Patrick for his signature. Within a year, Delia was named coexecutive director, and EPOCA geared up for its toughest fight yet—the Jobs Not Jails campaign.

Jobs Not Jails!

Cassandra Bensahih took a deep breath and looked out at the crowd of ten thousand gathered on Boston Common. The cold rain falling on April 26, 2014, evoked T. S. Eliot's line "April is the cruelest month." But here they were, nevertheless, ten thousand people chanting "Jobs Not Jails!" through intermittent showers.

Cassandra is a grandmother. She is a retired medical secretary. She is warm and hugs new acquaintances as surely as old friends. She is an African American woman who attends church regularly.

Cassandra is an addict. She's an ex-con. She's a black woman with a history of violence.

Through the help of Narcotics Anonymous (NA) and a supportive community of recovery, Cassandra left a world of crime and drugs and reconnected with her estranged family. "When I was in the grips of addiction," she recalled, "crime for profit seemed like a good idea. My family took a second place to my addiction, and it led me down the wrong road."

When it all caught up to her, Cassandra landed in jail, but she used prison as an opportunity to come clean—to herself, to her children, to society, to God. She began attending NA meetings, and upon completing a three-year sentence in 2010, Cassandra found new purpose volunteering with EPOCA after first encountering the group at a New Leaf workshop for returning citizens. As she learned about internalized racism in the criminal justice system, Cassandra recalled her youthful fascination with the civil rights movement and black-power icon Angela Davis, an advocate for women in prison.

Delia invited Cassandra to become an EPOCA leader, and then asked her to take on an internship. After proving herself a gifted organizer, Cassandra was offered an apprenticeship (a higher-level internship) and ultimately a job as a part-time organizer with EPOCA. The more she met 1:1 with other returning citizens, with clergy and community leaders, and with legislators at the Massachusetts State House, the more her passion for social justice reawakened, along with her self-esteem.

"Going to the State House—I never thought I'd do this," she said. "What was in the State House for me? Walking past the golden dome, that was like a lawyer's office to me! I didn't have any business up in there. I didn't even know what was going on inside—but now the governor knows who I am and most of the representatives. I built relationships with them, and I know them by face and name now."

Beginning in 2013, Cassandra started working the halls of the State House, promoting EPOCA's Jobs Not Jails initiative, along with a hundred coalition partners. In Massachusetts, mandatory minimum sentencing and a 2012 "3 strikes and you're out" law had created a growing demand for prisons and prison administration with no end in sight—all to be funded by taxpayers. The estimated cost of prison construction to meet the projected demand was over $2 billion. And at the same time as the Commonwealth prepared to add to its prison population, many returning citizens arrived back in their communities virtually unemployable. "The Scarlet X" impeded their full integration into society and encouraged a return to making a living through crime.

Cassandra, her colleagues in EPOCA, and Jobs Not Jails coalition partners seek to redirect the state's investments in public safety through three levels of institutional change. First, they advocate specific points of criminal justice reform. These alterations include the diversion of low-level drug offenders to treatment, even before trial, repealing mandatory minimum sentences, offering more job training and education for current inmates, and repealing the aforementioned "collateral sanctions."

Second, Jobs Not Jails aims to stop the prison construction demanded by high recidivism rates and mandatory minimum sentencing. EPOCA estimates the savings from a moratorium on prison construction at $2.3 billion, with a dividend of $150 million annually from maintenance expenses that would never be needed.

Third, the campaign calls for reinvesting the funds saved into jobs programs targeted at people living in high-crime areas of the state. In November 2014, California voters passed a similar measure through a referendum.

A year into the campaign, EPOCA needed a strong show of support from faith and community groups as well as returning citizens. Cassandra looked into the Jobs Not Jails crowd and saw faces familiar from hundreds of 1:1's over the past three years—ex-inmates, allies, even a politician or two. She kept the now-soaked crowd warm with jokes and stories, transitioning from speaker to musical act to speaker. She exhorted the crowd to return on April 30 to help hold up bright orange banners with thirty thousand petition signatures supporting Jobs Not Jails—enough to create a ribbon wrapped around the State House. At the peak of the rally, Cassandra introduced EPOCA colleague Donnell Wright, who organizes returning citizens in Springfield, Massachusetts.

At six feet, six inches, handsome and broad-shouldered, dressed impeccably in a three-piece suit, Donnell Wright looked more like one of the candidates for attorney general speaking at the rally than an ex-inmate. "We look real nice in a shirt and tie. Don't we?" he joked. The former inmates in the crowd laughed the loudest.

"Listen, people," he began, "This is very important, because the power is in the people. We have the power. We are here to change what's happening in Massachusetts. When I was sentenced for my offense, the judge told me, 'Mr. Wright, I wish I did not have to incarcerate you, sir, because you have done everything that we expected an individual to do, since you have been out on bail. But since you got yourself convicted of a crime that carried a minimum mandatory sentence, my hands are tied and I have to send you to jail.'"

Boos from the audience lasted longer than expected. He paused.

"But you know what? When he did send me to jail, I took every program that they had available and more."

The boos turned to cheers.

"I educated myself. While I was in prison, I earned the Massachusetts Real Estate License. I earned a Class B Commercial Truck Drivers License."

The cheers grew.

"I earned an associate degree in Business from Roxbury Community College. And also, I earned a bachelor of science degree from Boston University."

The crowd cheered as if Donnell was receiving his degree at this moment.

"But hold on. Guess what? Guess what I don't have? A job."

The cheers turned to boos, and the crowd settled down.

"Do you know why I don't have a job?" he continued. "Because I'm a convicted felon, and I'm a criminal, they say. I can't be reformed, and criminals never change, they say. So every time I apply for a job, I get the job, a good paying job. 'Oh, Mr. Wright, all your credentials are all in order. You have the degrees. You have all the accomplishments.' But then they do a CORI check, and they say, 'Mr. Wright, there's the door. Don't let it hit you on the way out.' So when we commit a crime and they incarcerate us, they tell us, 'Go into prison and rehabilitate yourself and go out and make something of yourself. Be a productive member of society.' But we all know when we get out, that doesn't happen. Does it?"

In unison, the onlookers yelled "No!"

"Because there are too many barriers to re-entry in Massachusetts. They don't want us to work. That's why the recidivism rate is 70 percent. Seven out of every ten individuals released from incarceration in this state will end up back in prison in the next ten years, and it's designed that way. I hope you will all join the 'Jobs, Not Jails' campaign, from here on out, and support our initiatives," he concluded. As the crowd cheered, Donnell introduced the first of two candidates for attorney general present. Both pledged their support for the campaign.

If Jobs Not Jails is to succeed, EPOCA will need to bring in even more faith-based and community partners. A crowd of ten thousand is not enough to move legislation so transformative. EPOCA's nascent partnership with the Society of St. Vincent de Paul offers some encouragement. Nationally, the Society seeks to work with returning citizens to meet basic needs but also to partner with them to transform social structures that promote recidivism and the ongoing cycle of poverty. The Massachusetts Vincentians comprise one of five statewide chapters who have partnered with Catholic Campaign for Human Development (CCHD)-funded organizations to work to dismantle The Scarlet "X."

In addition, EPOCA is looking at other means of job creation, apart from state investments. CCHD-funded Milk Not Jails in upstate New York offers one such model. Founder Tychist Baker had found a job in 2006 upon returning home from prison but was laid off, along with dozens of co-workers, in 2007. He remained unemployed for two years as the Great Recession set in. Finally, his friend, Lauren Melodia, proposed a novel idea. "You're trying to *find* a job, why not *make* a job?" she asked.

Tychist believed that the key to fighting recidivism is living-wage jobs, so with Lauren he created a worker-owned business that buys milk wholesale from family-owned dairy farms and then resells it to Community Supported Agriculture groups, and to consumers at farmers' markets. All four worker-owners are returning citizens. In five years, the business has grown to the point that Milk Not Jails now has its own office, car, and packaging. Five years from now, Tychist sees the company growing to twenty worker-owners, initiating sales to school districts, and serving as a pipeline from prison to work, a model EPOCA may someday imitate.

Organizing with Empathy

The Jobs Not Jails campaign would never have come so far without the relational organizing efforts of returning citizens like

Delia, Cassandra, and José Garcia, a former cocaine dealer who discovered a talent for advocacy at MCI-Norfolk. Mandatory minimum sentences hit José personally. Caught with over two hundred grams of cocaine, a judge sentenced José to fifteen years in prison with no option of parole. Like Donnell, José was an inmate who channeled his energy into self-improvement, earning a bachelor's degree in sociology from Boston University while incarcerated.

He also became involved with Families Against Mandatory Minimums (FAMM), a national organization formed in 1991 to reverse trends toward mandatory minimum sentences. Working from inside MCI-Norfolk, José organized inmates and their families. His special gift was ghostwriting letters to public officials for less articulate inmates and their families. "I started writing letters to send in to elected officials from our families out there," he said. "So our families would sign them and send the letters to their representatives, to support change on the mandatory minimum sentences. I sent over 5,300 letters—ten different types of support letters. While I was doing that, all the prisoners began to see me as a leader."

José quickly became the most popular inmate in MCI-Norfolk. Fellow prisoners urged him to run for the office of Latino president of the inmate governance council. Still remarkably racialized, the inmate council provided a voice for prisoners regarding day-to-day administrative matters. Various sectors of the prison elected council representatives, and a triumvirate of presidents—one black, one Latino, one white—led the council and its various committees: Legal, Visitation, Food, and more. For electoral purposes, Asians caucused with Latinos, and Native Americans, usually of mixed race, identified with their secondary racial group.

Latino inmates elected José as their president for his letter-writing abilities, but as president, José quickly realized he needed to develop new abilities that suited the job—particularly meeting skills. He devoured *Robert's Rules of Order*, quickly mastering parliamentary procedure. "It was interesting," he recalled, "I didn't know anything about that!" For the last years of his sentence, José stood unopposed as Latino president.

EPOCA was not the new world for José that it was for Delia and Cassandra. Policy and advocacy were passions he developed *inside* prison, along with a wonkish interest in meeting procedure. Organizing ex-inmates scattered on the outside proved different than organizing inmates living in tight quarters, however. Just identifying potential leaders could be complicated! But José kept his ears open for prison references among acquaintances, always responding to their stories with empathy.

"Yesterday," he said, "I went to the auto parts store and this guy was talking about how his friend got arrested, and he's going to face so many years, and I said, 'Oh, yeah, I did time in prison.' And it's like if someone knows you went through the same thing they are going through, it's easier for them to talk to you. If you haven't been to prison and they talk to you when they are coming out, they don't think you understand." José's work as an auto mechanic puts him in touch with people from all walks of life. He quickly picks up on the cues ex-inmates communicate. Sometimes he recognizes them from his fifteen years at MCI-Norfolk.

"Mocha" is one such ex-inmate. He and José became acquainted at MCI-Norfolk. Soon after Mocha's release, José identified him in downtown Worcester. "He looked kind of lost," José recalled. "So we started talking, and I learned he didn't have a job." José remembered Mocha's occasional conflicts with prison administration over treatment of inmates and his participation in various inmate movements. "So I told him about EPOCA," he said. "I took him to meet the EPOCA staff, and then I introduced him to all of the members, and he's been a part of EPOCA ever since. When we have to do a rally, whenever we have to do any outreach, he's there."

José organizes through his own web of relationships—people he knew in prison, acquaintances he meets through his work as an auto mechanic, even folks he runs into on the streets of Worcester. But personal relationships are not the only avenue bringing new leaders into EPOCA. Steve O'Neil, co-executive director and the only staff member who has not spent time in prison, explained that the richest source of EPOCA leaders is twelve-step recovery programs. "So many people have been convicted for crimes they committed when they were addicts. Once they're in Alcoholics Anonymous (AA) and Narcotics Anonymous or (NA), they want to get their life back on track and find jobs. EPOCA is there for them," he said.

A sizable number of EPOCA members attend twelve-step programs like AA and NA. When they meet a returning citizen who expresses dismay over their difficulties securing employment, EPOCA leaders invite him or her to one of the organization's biweekly Sunday afternoon membership meetings or to sign up for a New Leaf Program workshop.

The New Leaf Program, designed in collaboration with the Workforce Central Career Center in Worcester, provides return-ing citizens with the opportunity to demonstrate their abilities and prove themselves to a job counselor, who, when she or he believes the ex-inmate is ready, will match the job candidate with the right employer. When the match is made, the Workforce Central staff provides technical assistance to the employer to secure a $2,400 per employee tax credit and consulting regard-ing best practices to help the business and their new employee succeed together.

Many New Leaf graduates become intrigued with EPOCA and stay with the organization to work on campaigns like Jobs Not Jails. Others enter EPOCA after attending one of its work-shops on sealing criminal records, led in partnership with Greater Boston Legal Services. Sealing a record prevents most employers and landlords from seeing it. Common sealed records include first-time drug possession convictions and cases dismissed by a judge or concluded by a jury's "not guilty" finding. Both the New Leaf and the criminal record sealing workshops are ser-vices provided by EPOCA, but they are also pools of potential leaders. In this sense, EPOCA is like the Progress Center for

Independent Living (see Chapter 4). Important services draw in potential leaders, and current leaders who attend these gatherings then recruit those with the most leadership potential to attend organizing meetings.

The organizing process, as José demonstrated, is built on the experience of empathy. A person who has just been released from prison listens to another ex-inmate differently than he or she would a social worker or parole officer. They share common experiences of prison and, in most cases, addiction and recovery. Among EPOCA's leaders, one of the most successful empathetic organizers is Lilly Williams.

Like many EPOCA leaders, Lilly came to EPOCA through a recovery program called Everyday Miracles. "Someone over there was talking about CORI," she said. "She was telling me how you can get your record sealed, and they said you got to go over to EPOCA. I asked, 'What's EPOCA?' and they said, 'I don't know—you just got to go over there.' The first time I came, nobody answered, the second time I came, nobody answered, and I thought, 'What type of place is this??!! Nobody is never here!' [staff and leaders were out organizing]. So I went earlier and I found Steve (O'Neil) and a couple other volunteers here in the office. I walked in and I was like—WOW!—there was a spirit in the room, a good spirit—it was exhilarating, it was powerful! It was something that I had to be a part of."

Lilly did not join out of economic self-interest. Her profession at the time, beauty and hair styling, does not typically require criminal background checks, as barbers and beauticians are generally considered independent contractors who pay a "chair rental" fee to a shop owner. For Lilly, EPOCA fulfilled a deep need to help other people struggling with addictions and violence, a passion rooted in an unspeakable trauma—witnessing her own mother's murder.

"When I was four or five," she began, "my mom was killed by her boyfriend. She was brutally beaten. After he did everything that he wanted to—you know—he put us all in the bed together, and that's where I heard my mother take her last breaths.

The next morning, he got me ready to take me to his mother's house, and I asked, 'Why did you kill my mommy?' And he said, 'Because I wanted to work for her.' And I didn't understand. Still today, I don't."

Lilly went to live with her grandparents, who did their best. But she still grew up with a strong sense of inadequacy. When her grandparents died during her teenage years, she began to develop relationships with people who took advantage of and even abused her. Alcohol and illegal drugs offered some distraction and relief. "After my guidance was taken away, no one guided me," she said. "I basically had to guide myself. I made a lot of mistakes, because, you know, a lot of phony guidance came into my life."

Drugs led to prostitution and violence. Lilly was arrested for soliciting, disorderly conduct, public drunkenness, assault and battery, and possession of illegal drugs. At first, judges sentenced her to short stints in jail or rehab. But ultimately, they tired of seeing her in court and sentenced Lilly, now in her forties, to three months at MCI-Framingham.

"I remember they took me to E-block," she said, "and when I walked in, I looked up and I seen bars from the top, and another set at the bottom and I started crying. I was like, 'Oh, my God. I am in jail.' You know? Like it hit me, like, 'You're in jail. This is the real thing here.' And I cried and I cried. One lady said to me, she said, 'You're going to be okay.' And I'm saying to myself, 'How the heck am I going to be okay? I'm in jail.' And I was in a cell with this other lady and she was in there for drug trafficking. This woman did not know when she was going to get out. At least I had a date. Outside our cell, I never will forget this, there was this Pepsi-Cola machine and the only thing I could think about was getting out and having a drink of that Pepsi. I was like, 'Lord, if I can get out and drink a soda, I will never come back in here.'"

In the soft illumination of the Pepsi machine, Lilly began to take stock of her life. "At the same time, my son was in another prison," she continued. "So we were corresponding with each other. You know, that really had an impact on me. Like, 'What the heck are you doing?' And finally dealing with my mother's death and all of the abuse, it just broke me—I gave up. I was tired of fighting."

The first step: "We admitted we were powerless." Lilly began a journey into recovery, attending prison AA and NA meetings. Upon release, however, she strode right past that Pepsi machine. Ultimately, it was only a symbol. What she would go on to obtain was the *real* reward behind the symbol—the freedom to live outside the prison of addiction and abusive relationships.

Shortly after her first encounter with EPOCA in 2012, Lilly began to set up 1:1's with other ex-inmates, often the newly released. She discovered she had more in common with these returning citizens than she ever imagined. Not only were they receptive to her and the vision of EPOCA, but many also looked to her for advice. She loved connecting the various people she met and convening meetings.

"I'm a good listener," she explained, "and I listen for what you're passionate about. I listen for what affects you. And I might need you to work with me to move this mountain. I know you are passionate about having to move this mountain, so I come to you and say, I want to move that mountain. You want to come with me so we can do this together? And you can say, 'Yes, Lilly, we can do this together, and I know Joe over here. I can bring him over.'"

After eighteen months of mentoring Lilly, Steve invited her to become an EPOCA intern, ramping up both her commitment and the number of 1:1's she completed each month. At first she was apprehensive. "Having a title brought up all that old stuff because I didn't think I was good enough to do it." But Lilly's experience of a lifetime of trauma and abuse proved to be an *asset* within EPOCA, not a liability. Returning citizens *wanted* to open up to her and hear what she had to say.

One EPOCA member Lilly mentored was a woman named Brenda. They hit it off well in part because of the similarities in their life stories. Lilly took Brenda under her wing and, after a time, took her on formal outreaches to returning citizens. Brenda performed well. "She knew the paperwork that we needed and she knew how to put an outreach package together," Lilly recalled. "I seen how she got the enjoyment and it made her feel good about herself. So I would say to her, 'Brenda, we are going on an outreach on so-and-so date. Can you get the package together?' Then on that date, I said, 'Brenda, can we get the paperwork together?' It would already be done. She's like, 'Lilly, I'm ahead of you on that one.' You know? Yes!"

Soon, Brenda began to coach a bemused Lilly. "She'd be like, 'Don't forget to do this. Don't forget to do that,'" said Lilly. "I mean, everything that's supposed to be done, from A to Z, this woman took charge of and made sure I was on the right page. So now the student had become the teacher. You know? Then I would let her do the openings, when we would go out—and tell them what EPOCA is about, or sometimes I would let her close it up. The job that she would do, the way she presented herself. The passion that she had, telling them about what she did and what she was doing within the organization. It was like a light bulb went off in this woman. You know? It was like new life, where there was a flower withered, now it bloomed. It came to life."

Lilly may as well have been talking about herself—the light bulb, the flower, the new life. Within EPOCA she is shining, she is growing—and others have noticed. In September 2014, the day before our second interview, a Worcester community health agency hired Lilly as a weekend drug and alcohol counselor, her first position in human services.

Lilly showed little emotion when I asked her how she felt about the new job. "This is the beginning of a brand new phase in my life, you know?" she said. "I'm looking forward to it." Then she began to cry:

> I really am. I know that God has bigger plans for me. You know? I just want to be available for the people and do for someone what wasn't done for me. You know? Because there's so many people out there. So many good

people that's broken. They are so broken and the only thing they're looking for is somebody to understand and talk to them; somebody to make them feel whole, like a person. You know? That's all I was looking for. I was looking for someone to love me. So I'm able to do it for other people. And to help that woman who is being brutally beaten right now. I remember my mother being beaten and I was looking, and her predator made me watch him have sex with my mom. There's so many women who go through that and don't even know that there's a way out. You know? Some lose their life. Some are scarred for life. So I want to be that person to help heal some of that.

Beyond Empowerment

Lilly's story, like Delia's, Cassandra's, and José's, is a chronicle of Integral Human Development. True, EPOCA helped each come to terms with her or his own *power*, but if you ask these leaders how their lives are different today because of EPOCA, they would point to their development as *people*. God created each to be a unique person, but trauma, abuse, drugs, and struggles with poverty hid that person away. Today, these women and men do not conceal who they are. If you ask, they will tell you about their experience of incarceration and reentry, but they will also insist that you come to know the whole of their personhood. They are not boxes to be checked with a Scarlet "X"—they are human beings, created in the image and likeness of God, who made mistakes, paid for those errors, and now want nothing more than a chance to pursue happiness and sit at the table of public life.

If you travel Massachusetts Route 9 east from EPOCA's office in Worcester, through the upscale suburbs of Newton and Brookline, Massachusetts, you will eventually cross into Boston, the setting of Hawthorne's *The Scarlet Letter*. The novel tells the story of Hester Prynne's forbidden seventeenth-century affair with a young Puritan minister, Rev. Arthur Dimmesdale. Their liaison comes to light when she bears a child, despite her husband's long absence overseas. Hester will not reveal the name of her lover and is sentenced to a public shaming and forced to wear a scarlet "A" on her chest.

Long ostracized, Hester began a life of charitable works after Rev. Dimmesdale and her vengeful husband died. As time passed, Hawthorne wrote, the same townspeople who once condemned Hester not only forgave her trespass, but actually sought her counsel:

> [A]s Hester Prynne had no selfish ends, nor lived in any measure for her own profit and enjoyment, people brought all their sorrows and perplexities, and besought her counsel, as one who had herself gone through a mighty trouble. Women, more especially—in the continually recurring trials of wounded, wasted, wronged, misplaced, or erring and sinful passion—or with the dreary burden of a heart unyielded, because unvalued and unsought came to Hester's cottage, demanding why they were so wretched, and what the remedy! Hester comforted and counseled them, as best she might. She assured them, too, of her firm belief that, at some brighter period, when the world should have grown ripe for it, in Heaven's own time, a new truth would be revealed.[6]

Lilly, José, Cassandra, and Delia reveal a portion of this "new truth," a vision of reconciliation tied to a pragmatic way forward—removing the stigma of a criminal record and the mandatory minimum sentences that drive excessive incarceration. These returning citizens teach us how to divest from the prison-industrial complex, while reinvesting in living-wage jobs. Most of all, they help us fully comprehend that "new truth" also found in Catholic teaching on human life: we are better than our worst actions, and the dignity of the person—fashioned in the image and likeness of God—can ultimately triumph over our worst frailties.

Afterword:
The End of Our Pilgrimage

Not far from the colonial cemetery where Hester Prynne and Rev. Dimmesdale are said to be laid to rest lies Boston Harbor (Chapter 6). What better location to complete our pilgrimage than that shrine of American democracy where the Boston Tea Party helped to spark the American Revolution? The Sons of Liberty and the men of Irish, Scottish, French, Portuguese, and African descent who joined them in dumping a shipment of British tea into the bay were not protesting the monarchy in general or the issue of taxes on tea specifically. They denounced "taxation without representation" and called for full participation in their own governance—in short, they demanded subsidiarity and a role in public life.

Paul Revere and his Sons of Liberty were not so different from the women and men we have met on this pilgrimage with the Catholic Campaign for Human Development (CCHD). Consider Coy Verdin and the Native American and Cajun shrimpers of Louisiana bayou country (Chapter 1), denied a seat at the table where decisions are made about flood control and coastal restoration, or Guadalupe Santana of central Washington State (Chapter 2), approaching her state representative about a problematic standardized test, only to be told he could not intervene because he was not in office when the legislature first mandated the test. In what ways are their stories *not* taxation without representation?

161

"We are just asking for what everybody else is getting," declared Henry Boyce of Progress Center (Chapter 4), echoing Pope Francis's appeal for all of the "excluded." From the low-wage laborers of Interfaith Worker Justice's workers centers (Chapter 3) to the returning citizens of EPOCA, to the at-risk young adults of Café Reconcile (Chapter 1), the leaders of CCHD-funded organizations call for modest yet somehow radical outcomes—to be treated as a subject, not an object, a person, not a thing, a child of God, not a monster. With each of these new assignations comes *power*—the ability to act—and a transformation from excluded to empowered.

Yet throughout our journey, empowerment has been only part of the story. The larger narrative remains Integral Human Development. Recall Cissimarie Juan and Sterling Johnson newly encountering and then embracing their ancestral culture (Chapter 5), Spic and Span domestic workers sharing their wage theft settlement in solidarity with a co-worker prevented by legal technicalities from receiving any funds (Chapter 3), and a woman choosing life in the supportive embrace of a Seattle Women's Justice Circle (Chapter 2). Each of these stories—and an abundance of others within each chapter—reveal that the true fruit of CCHD lies far beyond empowerment.

Perhaps you've been inspired by these stories, and you want to know what you can do. In many ways, you need look no further than the Parable of the Good Samaritan. You know the story: a "scholar of the Law," or religious lawyer, approaches Jesus in Luke 10:25–37, asking, "What must I do to inherit everlasting life?" The lawyer seems more intent on trapping Jesus in a theological error than improving his own spiritual life. So Jesus throws the question back at him. The lawyer replies,

> "You shall love the Lord your God with all your heart and all your soul, and with all your strength, and with all your mind; and your neighbor as yourself." And [Jesus] said to him, "You have given the right answer; do this, and you

will live." But wanting to justify himself, he asked Jesus, "And who is my neighbor?"

Jesus responds with the parable we know so well. A Levite, a temple priest, and a Samaritan all encounter a wounded crime victim, abandoned for dead on the side of the road. The first two pass the bloodied man, prohibited by Jewish purity codes from touching the "unclean" victim. The Samaritan comes next. He binds the man's wounds, takes him to an inn, and pays the innkeeper to care for the wounded man until he returns. Jesus asks the lawyer, "Who was neighbor to the man?" The scholar correctly answers, "The one who showed him mercy."

We often focus on the primary lesson of the parable: love and compassion are the supreme law, but within the story is also a powerful example of crossing social borders to accomplish the will of God. Samaritans were members of an ethnic group despised by the Jews of the day. Moved by charity, the Samaritan helped a man who he might well assume hated him. By making the Samaritan the hero of the story, Jesus turns the social conventions of the time on their head and provides us with a model for responding to the marginalized.

Who are those people living on the margins in the United States? They are people with disabilities, Americans living within the borders of Native American nations, youth raised in troubled families and surrounded by violence, low-wage workers, unauthorized migrants and ex-prisoners. They live just beyond the social borders of our own lives. When, like the Good Samaritan, we cross these social boundaries to respond to injustice and human need with love, we commit acts of solidarity.

As Pope Francis put it, "[t]he word 'solidarity' is a little worn and at times poorly understood, but it refers to something more than a few sporadic acts of generosity. It presumes the creation of a new mindset which thinks in terms of community and the priority of the life of all over the appropriation of goods by a few. . . . learned with the humble, the poor, the sick and all those who are on the existential peripheries of life."[1] Let us now offer a prayer for God's help to live in solidarity with the excluded, in the words of Archbishop Dom Helder Camara of Brazil:

> Do not smile and say
> you are already with us.
> Millions do not know you
> And to us who do,
> what is the difference?
> What is the point of your presence
> if our lives do not alter?
> Change our lives,
> shatter our complacency.
> Make your word
> flesh of our flesh,
> blood of our blood
> and our life's purpose.
> Take away the quietness
> of a clear conscience.
> Press us uncomfortably.
> For only thus is
> that other peace made,
> your peace.[2]

Notes

Introduction

[1] Catholic Campaign for Human Development, "Our Mission," Poverty USA, http://www.povertyusa.org/our-mission/about-cchd/.

[2] *Merriam-Webster. Online Dictionary*, http://www.merriam-webster.com/dictionary/empower.

[3] Michael Gecan, *Going Public* (Boston: Beacon Press, 2002), 36–37.

[4] Pope Francis, *The Joy of the Gospel* (Frederick, MD: Word Among Us Press, 2013), no. 181.

[5] Pope Paul VI, *On the Development of Peoples*, no. 14, www.vatican.va.

[6] Ibid., no. 3.

[7] *Catechism of the Catholic Church*. 2nd ed. (Washington, DC: United States Catholic Conference, 1997), no. 1939.

[8] Pope Benedict XVI, *Caritas in Veritate* (San Francisco: Ignatius Press, 2009), no. 19.

[9] Pope Francis, "Fraternity, the Foundation and Pathway to Peace." 2014 World Day of Peace Message, no 4, www.vatican.va.

[10] Pope Benedict, no. 18.

[11] Ibid., no. 24.

[12] Ibid., no. 38.

Chapter 1

[1] Peirce Lewis, *New Orleans: The Making of an Urban Landscape* (New York: Center for American Places, 2003).

[2] Bill Quigley, "Katrina Pain Index 2013: New Orleans Eight Years Later," *Huffington Post*. August 27, 2013, http://www.huffingtonpost.com/.

[3] Café Reconcile, "Why Reconcile," http://cafereconcile.org.

[4] Nathaniel Rich, "The Most Ambitious Environmental Lawsuit Ever," *New York Times Magazine*, October 2, 2014, www.nytimes.com.

[5] Barbara Corbelini Duarte, "Restoration Plan for Fast Eroding Louisiana Coast Lacks Funds," *NY Times*, May 24, 2014, http://nola14.nytimes-institute.com.

Chapter 2

[1] Deb Came and Lisa Ireland, *Graduation and Dropout Statistics Annual Report 2011–2012* (Olympia, WA: Washington State Office of Superintendent of Public Instruction, 2012), http://www.k12.wa.us.

[2] Algernon Austin. "No Relief in 2012 from High Unemployment for African Americans and Latinos," Economic Policy Institute, February 16, 2012, www.epi.org.

[3] SESRC–Puget Sound Division, Kyra Kester, and Candiya Mann, *Bullying in Washington Schools* (Olympia: Washington State University, 2008), 28, https://www.k12.wa.us/safetycenter/BullyingHarassment/pubdocs/BullyinginWashingtonSchools.pdf.

Chapter 3

[1] Annette Bernhardt, Ruth Milkman, Nik Theodore et al., *Broken Laws, Unprotected Workers: Violations of Employment and Labor Laws in America's Cities* (Chicago: Center for Urban Economic Development, 2009), 13.

[2] Ibid., 15.

[3] Ibid., 42–43.

[4] Ibid., 44–45.

[5] Ibid., 46.

[6] Ibid., 42–46.

[7] Ibid., 5.

[8] Ibid., 23.

[9] Ibid., 3.

[10] Government Accountability Office, *Wage and Hour Division's Complaint Intake and Investigative Processes Leave Low Wage Workers Vulnerable to Wage Theft* (Washington, DC: Government Accountability Office, 2009), 2, 4, 11.

[11] Ibid., 5–7, 9–10.

[12] Ibid.

[13] Ibid., 10.

[14] Ibid., 15–16.

[15] Ibid.

[16] Ibid., 23.

[17] Ibid., 22.

[18] Craig K. Elwell, "Inflation and the Real Minimum Wage: A Fact Sheet," Congressional Research Service. January 8, 2014, https://www.fas.org/sgp/crs/misc/R42973.pdf.

[19] Maricela Flores, "Unprecedented Victory for Low Wage Workers," www.chipsterlife.com.

[20] U.S. Chamber of Commerce, "U.S. Chamber Report Profiles Five Leading Worker Centers at the Forefront of New Union Organizing Push," February 26, 2014, www.uschamber.com.

[21] U.S. Chamber of Commerce, *The New Model of Representation: An Overview of Leading Workers Centers* (Washington, DC: U.S. Chamber of Commerce, 2014.), 2.

[22] Ibid.

[23] Ibid., 23.

[24] Ibid., 22.

[25] Ibid., 23.

[26] Ibid., 22.

[27] Steve Striffler, "Undercover in a Chicken Factory," *Utne Reader*, January/February 2004, http://www.utne.com.

[28] Pope Francis, *Message of His Holiness Francis for the Celebration of the World Day of Peace*, January 1, 2014, http://w2.vatican.va.

Chapter 4

[1] Saint John Paul II, *Laborem Exercens*, no. 3 (1981), http://www.vatican.va.

[2] Ibid., no. 13.

[3] United States Conference of Catholic Bishops, "Two Feet of Love in Action," http://www.usccb.org.

[4] Ibid.

[5]   U.S. Bureau of the Census,"Nearly 1 in 5 People Have a Disability in the U.S.," *Census Newsroom*, https://www.census.gov.

[6]   Phil Rockrohr, "First Residents Arrive at Newly Opened Grove Apartments in Former Comcast Building," *Oak Park Sun Times,* December 1, 2013, http://oakpark.suntimes.com.

Chapter 5

[1]   2011 data, obtained from the U.S. Department of Health and Human Services, http://minorityhealth.hhs.gov4.

[2]   National Institutes for Health, "The Pima Indians: Obesity and Diabetes," http://diabetes.niddk.nih.gov.

[3]   Louie Carl, "Childhood Obesity within Tohono O'odham Schools," *IHS Public Health Newsletter for Indian Health Services Tucson Area (San Xavier, Sells, San Simon, and Santa Rosa)* 1 (July 2010): 1–2.

[4]   Mission InSite, Full InSite Report, based on U.S. Census and Experian data. Generated February 2, 2014, by Chuck Salter, president, Mission InSite.

[5]   Arizona Rural Policy Institute, Center for Business Outreach, W.A. Franke College of Business, Northern Arizona, *Demographic Analysis of the Tohono O'odham Nation Using 2010 Census and 2010 American Community Survey Estimates* (Sells, AZ: Department of Planning and Economic Development, Tohono O'odham Nation Tribe, 2012), 33–38.

[6]   Teri Woods, Karen Blaine, and Lauri Francisco, "O'odham Himdag as a Source of Strength and Wellness," *Journal of Sociology and Social Welfare* 29 (March 2002): 48.

[7]   Laura Marble, "The Tohono O'odham Fight Diabetes with Crops Their Grandparents Grew," *Explorer News*, November 29, 2006.

[8]   Arizona Department of Commerce, *Economy of the Tohono O'odham Nation* (Tempe, AZ: Arizona State University W. P. Carey School of Business Center for Competitiveness and Prosperity Research, L. William Seidman Research Institute, 2008).

[9]   Published by TOCA, *From l'Itoi's Garden* is available at www.blurb.com and www.tocaonline.org.

Chapter 6

[1] Michelle Rodriguez, Natividad Rodriguez, and Maurice Emsellem, *"65 Million 'Need Not Apply": The Case for Reforming Criminal Background Checks for Employment* (New York: National Employment Law Project, 2011), 3.

[2] U.S. Department of Labor, "Complying with Nondiscrimination Provisions: Criminal Record Restrictions and Discrimination Based on Race and National Origin," ADM Notice, no. 306, January 29, 2013, www.dol.gov/ofccp/regs/compliance/directives/dir306.htm#ftn4.

[3] S. Adams, "Background Checks on Job Candidates: Be Very Careful," *Forbes.com*, www.forbes.com/sites/susanadams/2013/06/21/background-checks-on-job-candidates-be-very-careful/.

[4] Devah Pager, Bruce Western, and Naomi Sugie, "Sequencing Disadvantage: Barriers to Employment Facing Young Black and White Men with Criminal Records," *Annals of the Academy of Political and Social Science* 623, no. 1 (May 2009):195–213.

[5] Rodriguez, 1–2.

[6] Nathaniel Hawthorne, *The Scarlet Letter*, 315.

Afterword

[1] Pope Francis, Address to the Participants in the Plenary Assembly of the International Union of Superiors General (UISG), May 8, 2013, http://www.vatican.va.

[2] Archbishop Dom Helder Camara, *The Desert Is Fertile* (Maryknoll, NY: Orbis Books, 1974).

Index

Numbers in italics indicate images.